Sharks in the Shallows

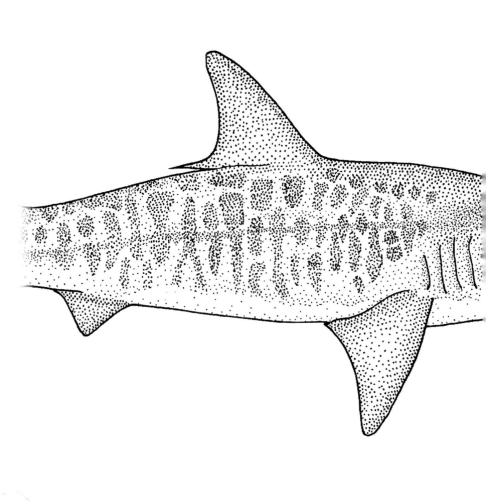

SHARKS

in the
SHALLOWS

Attacks on the Carolina Coast

W. Clay Creswell   FOREWORD BY MARIE LEVINE

THE UNIVERSITY OF
SOUTH CAROLINA PRESS

Published by the University of South Carolina Press
Columbia, South Carolina 29208

www.uscpress.com

Manufactured in the United States of America

30 29 28 27 26 25 24 23 22 21
10 9 8 7 6 5 4 3 2

Library of Congress Cataloging-in-Publication Data
can be found at http://catalog.loc.gov/.

ISBN: 978-1-64336-180-2 (paperback)
ISBN: 978-1-64336-181-9 (ebook)

Frontispiece: Tiger shark, illustration by Elise Pullen

This book is dedicated with love to my sister, Cary Duncan.

CONTENTS

FOREWORD

Do you swim, surf, or dive in North or South Carolina? If so, this landmark book is for you. Long overdue, it is a culmination of decades of research on unanticipated human interactions with sharks in the Carolinas, and it could have only been written by W. Clay Creswell.

The research presented in this book is of enormous interest not only to scientists but also to historians, lifeguards, surfers, divers, swimmers, and everyone who wants to learn more about shark–human interactions. Clay's in-depth research highlights the causal factors involved in some unfortunate accidents and also illustrates just how seldom sharks injure humans. His recommendations on how to protect marine resource users from shark–human accidents can significantly lower the risk of a shark bite and should be implemented by all coastal municipalities.

The Shark Research Institute sponsors and conducts research on sharks and promotes their conservation. For many decades the Shark Research Institute has also maintained one of the largest worldwide databases of shark attacks for medical professionals, known today as the *Global Shark Attack File* (www.sharkattackfile .net). Years ago Clay began contributing data on negative shark–human interactions in the Carolinas, and his meticulous research remains unparalleled.

Today sharks are being exterminated at an unprecedented rate; they are being killed faster than they can reproduce, primarily for their fins or caught as bycatch. It is estimated that seventy-three million to one hundred million sharks are being slaughtered annually. Sharks have a vital role in the ocean ecosystem—the ecosystem that sustains you, me, and everyone else on this planet. While the fear of sharks still afflicts some people as a result of the negative (and erroneous) image created by *Jaws,* the good news is that today more and more people recognize the value of these amazing animals and are working to ensure their survival.

Marie Levine, PhD
Founder, Shark Research Institute
Princeton, New Jersey

PREFACE

We were not alone among the rolling waves in the ocean that day.

The possibility of danger concealed just under the murky green-brown surf was not on my mind that sunny July afternoon in 1993. In my early twenties, I was vacationing at Long Beach, North Carolina (on Oak Island), as my family had done since my childhood. The beach was fairly crowded, and a few family members, friends, and I were wading approximately waist deep. We had been in the warm, salty water for nearly an hour when suddenly a shock wave of fear shot through me as I felt the slick, smooth strength of something meeting my outer left thigh. Despite lasting mere seconds, I remember thinking that whatever it was felt heavy, resembling a log riding a gentle subsurface current. Instinctively I jolted out of the immediate area, alerting my group. No one else seemed too worried about it though, so I tried to shrug it off as the staggering weight of my fear melted into a lingering feeling of uneasiness. Shortly afterward a friend in our group also felt something bump his leg, and he too moved quickly from the area where he was standing. The feeling of eeriness seemed to creep its way onto the others now, coloring us all with the sense of being uncomfortably exposed in the waist-deep opaqueness below the surface. When the same man in our group was bumped a second time, his reaction of panic had all of us scurrying for shore.

We will never know exactly what grazed against us that summer, but whatever it was took away our desire to reenter the surf for the rest of the day. It has remained ingrained in my memory, becoming yet another contributing factor to a lifelong fascination with the shadows in the shallows—especially those in my local waters—swimming just below the surface, unseen, yet sometimes felt.

$\approx$

North and South Carolina, where I have served as an investigator
of marine animal bite incidents involving humans for the past fourteen years, are home to a great variety of coastal localities, ideal for
those searching for a vacation getaway or desiring to live the salt
life year-round. Whether you are looking for small coastal communities filled with southern charm, pristine secluded barrier island
beaches, or strands strewn with amusement parks, restaurants, and
live entertainment, the Carolinas offer it all. Every year millions of
people travel to these Carolina paradises in search of sand, sun, fun,
and surf. From North Carolina's northernmost beach destination,
Knott's Island, to South Carolina's southernmost barrier island,
Daufuskie Island, 500 miles of coastline offer vintage, nationally
recognized ocean boardwalks and boast some of the oldest seaside
resort areas in America. The common thread linking these diverse
destinations is the plentiful stretch of soft, sandy beaches border-
ing some of the most inviting waters the Atlantic Ocean has to offer. Year-round, visitors and residents alike enjoy the waters of the
Carolinas for their beautiful swimming and surfing environments,
world-class fishing, famous dive sites, and plentiful boating, canoe-
ing, and kayaking opportunities.

Not only are the shallow estuaries, sounds, and ocean waters of
the Carolinas appealing to those of us who love the beach, but they
also provide a healthy natural habitat for a variety of marine wildlife. Many species of fish and invertebrates thrive in Carolina waters throughout their entire lives—from tideland areas to offshore
locations. The shallow coastal zone waters of the Carolinas routinely
boast commercially important species of shellfish and crustaceans
such as blue crabs, oysters, and shrimp—as well as fish species,
including red drum, spotted sea trout, flounder, and sheepshead.
Other species enter Carolina seaside areas primarily to spawn. All
of these animals contribute to a vast marine ecosystem that is part
of an intricate and valuable food web. At the top of this vast underwater ecosystem remains a group of fish that have become some
of the most notorious of all the world's apex predators, instilling
a deep seed of exaggerated and undeserved fear and hatred in the
minds of millions of people who live, work, visit, and play by the sea.

These great fish are the sharks.

1 Sharks of the Carolinas

Worldwide, approximately 500 identified shark species exist today, and around fifty-six of those species reside seasonally or year-round in the Carolinas.[1] These Carolina dwellers range in size from the largest fish in the world—the *whale shark,* which can reach lengths of forty feet—to the small broadband lantern shark, which measures a mere thirteen inches. The warmth of the diverse offshore and nearshore ocean waters—as well as the brackish sounds, estuaries, and coastal rivers of the Carolinas—are ideal for sharks in that they provide good shelter and a vast variety of food. Some species—including smooth and spiny dogfish, Atlantic sharpnose, blacknose, blacktip, sandbar, tiger, dusky, and bull sharks—use Carolina sounds and estuaries as nurser habitats to either pup their young or as areas where young sharks temporarily reside. The following Carolina locations are all documented nursing grounds utilized by sharks—in South Carolina: St. Helena Sound, North Edisto Bay, Charleston Harbor, Winyah Bay, and Bulls Bay; in North Carolina: the Cape Fear River, Ocracoke Inlet, Hatteras Inlet, Pamlico Sound, and Oregon Inlet.

The Importance of Sharks

Have you considered how much we depend on the ocean for our survival? Oceans cover nearly three-quarters of the earth's surface and provide most of its water supply. Oceans also produce over half of the oxygen that we breathe and absorb a large amount of carbon dioxide from our planet's atmosphere. They transport heat from the equator to the poles, which regulates our climate and weather patterns. And oceans provide around one-third of the world's food supply.[2]

Sharks—some of which are even considered *apex predators* (i.e., at the peak of all other species)—bring health and balance to our oceans by keeping populations of various crustaceans, fish, marine reptiles, and marine mammals at a normal, healthy level. They also play a key role in keeping our oceans free of disease by preying on sick and dying creatures and scavenging the carcasses of already deceased animals at sea, including those that wash into the oceans from rivers.

But when most people think about sharks, they do not think about the beneficial fish that keep our oceans clean. Instead, the creature in the movie *Jaws* comes to mind. Who would not be horrified at the thought of a monstrous fish lurking somewhere close by, possibly just a few feet away from an unsuspecting swimmer? Although this mental picture is usually exaggerated in people's minds, the fact is that sharks have been known to "attack"—or, to be more specific, to bite people from time to time—usually doing so by mistake and often leaving the area immediately following the bite. But this one shark trait—their occasional tendency to launch attacks on humans—generates more attention and interest from the general public than any other aspect of their behavior.

In the writing of this book, I do not intend to portray any shark species in a negative way. I love sharks, and they really are some of the most misunderstood and mischaracterized creatures on the planet. As a result of this misinformation, people have attempted—throughout history and in many locations throughout the world—to rid the waters of sharks by the indiscriminate use of longlines and nets as well as through organized shark hunts. In the post-*Jaws* 1970s and 1980s, many recreational pier fishermen in the Carolinas possessed the attitude of "the only good shark is a dead shark" and would kill even young, harmless species such as Atlantic sharpnose and bonnetheads. During that period, I recall seeing fishermen bash the heads of hooked young sharks on pier railings and toss them on deck to rot in the sun—other sharks met a similarly gruesome fate, with fishermen just throwing them on the pier to slowly die. When possible, I would take those that didn't get their heads bashed and toss them over the side, back into the ocean.

With time, however, this societal attitude has increasingly changed for the better, thanks in large part to advances in not only shark research but also in modes of sharing the latest scientific information with the public through magazine and journal articles, publications on the Internet, and creative documentaries. Sharks are finally starting to gain support from a sector of the public who sees them in a more positive and realistic light for what they truly are—a very necessary and vulnerable group of animals that play an invaluable role in our marine environment. I hope that those who read this book will not see a horror story within these pages but instead will become more aware of safer ways in which we, as humans, can share the sharks' environment and learn something positive about their behavior. We should not fear sharks to the point of avoiding the water, nor should we choose to swim with, feed, or touch some of the bigger, more dangerous species to prove that they are naturally nonaggressive toward humans (even if this is usually true). All sharks, regardless of size, should be admired, appreciated, and respected for their beauty, for their survivability, for the important role that they play in the world, for their unpredictability, and for the capabilities they possess as wild apex predators.

Shark Fishing in the Carolinas

Sharks have historically been so plentiful in the Carolinas that established shark fishing businesses once flourished (until local and state governments implemented necessary stringent regulations for the protection of the species, making these business operations impractical). We have much to learn about shark reproduction habits; however, the fact remains that some species are vulnerable to extinction due to their slow growth rate, later-in-life sexual maturity, and tendency to bear only a few offspring at a time. According to Professor Frank J. Schwartz, a well-respected shark expert with the University of North Carolina (UNC) Institute of Marine Sciences in Morehead City:

> From 1918 to 1922 Cape Lookout Beaufort Ocean Leather Corporation had a viable shark fishery with catches of sharks up to seven feet in length at a rate of 50–60 a day were average. The years 1936–1941 saw a small shark fishery activated in Morehead City and in its prime, there was a reported 3,000 catches of

sharks over six feet long during a three-month season. [During the years] 1983–1985 a final small shark fishery longline operation emerged in Morehead City and ran with much success until it shut down.[3]

Sharks have also contributed heavily to fish catches hooked from boats, piers, and the surf in both Carolinas, with recorded landings dating back as far as 1874. After the 1975 release of *Jaws,* society spotlighted sharks to a greater extent in the public eye; thus, sharks became a more popular fishing target for laymen, serious hunters, and professional fishermen. Shark fishing clubs sprouted up along the East Coast, and some of these clubs fished Carolina waters for their trophies. The annual Poor Boy Shark Tournament at Hughes Marina in Shallotte, North Carolina, was popular from 1982 until its demise in 1996. During this event anywhere from six to twenty boats of experienced shark fishermen would head seaward, usually at night, to hunt sharks for three 24-hour fishing days. Fishermen caught hundreds of sharks of various species during the tournament's heyday, with the largest being a thirteen-foot tiger shark that weighed 939 pounds.[4]

The Carolinas lay claim to several large shark catches that include a twelve-foot tiger shark hooked and released from the beach on Topsail Island, North Carolina, in 2016; a 421-pound state-record lemon shark taken from the Kure Beach Pier in North Carolina in 1978; and a 610-pound dusky shark landed from Jennette's Pier in Nags Head, North Carolina, in 1962. The greatest catch from the Carolinas, however, happened on June 14, 1964, when local shark fisherman Walter Maxwell landed a world-record tiger shark off the Cherry Grove Fishing Pier in South Carolina. Weighing in at 1,780 pounds, this shark measured almost fourteen feet in length and 103 inches in girth. The shark had to be weighed the morning after it was landed; therefore an estimated 10 percent of its actual weight was lost due to dehydration. Experts say that had someone weighed it when Maxwell had caught it, the shark would have tipped the scales at a ton. On the day before he caught this fish, Maxwell hooked but did *not* land an even bigger tiger shark off the same pier. According to Maxwell, "the one that got away" was long enough to have nearly overlapped the pier's end. Jim Michie, another experienced shark fisherman and Maxwell's fishing partner that day, estimated that the shark was around eighteen feet long. Both men say that they thought the shark weighed at least 2,500 pounds. Maxwell also landed the North Carolina state-record tiger shark in 1966 off the Yaupon Pier at Oak Island. This catch is now known as the "YB Tiger," and a replica of the giant is on permanent display at the Yaupon Pier. Some sources inaccurately report the length of this state-record tiger shark, but I feel confident that my personal telephone conversation with Maxwell's wife confirms the actual measurements of this great catch: "YB Jaws," as people have also dubbed it, weighed in at 1,150 pounds, was twelve feet in length, and was seventy-seven inches in girth.[5]

On yet another occasion, Maxwell had his line hooked into a large 1,200-pound tiger shark when suddenly he witnessed the largest shark he had ever seen. The giant zeroed in on his hooked tiger shark and took a chunk of it that measured 36 inches across. From examining the size of the wound and the shape of the tooth impressions, Maxwell estimated that the attacker was most likely a great white shark in the 3,500-pound range.[6]

2 Summers of the Sharks
When Sharks Attack

Human existence as we know it depends largely on the survival of our sharks and the ecosystem in which they reside. With protections in place, and regulations limiting the hunting of some species and banning the taking of others, it seemed as though policymakers finally recognized the fact that we need sharks. These regulations on shark fishing have given this group of animals greater opportunity to thrive and replenish their populations as nature intended. Yet, despite growing awareness of sharks' value and importance to the world, they still have yet to overcome one major hurdle—our instinctive human fear of the unknown, the unseen, and the dangerous. Fear is a hardwired survival mechanism and is triggered in potentially unsafe and threatening situations. The year 2015 was known as *the summer of the shark*. It was an especially unusual year for the North Carolina coast, where a series of severe shark bites took place, some occurring in locations where shark attacks had never before been reported. Media coverage of these shark attacks capitalized on people's general fears, fueling public concern to the point that some people may have thought that the North Carolina coast was suffering from a shark attack epidemic.

The reality of 2015 is that it *was* a year in which shark bite incidents briefly spiked, not only in the Carolinas but worldwide. This was a natural pattern spike, as it is normal for some years to have higher numbers of incidents than others. Causes for this increase can include warmer water temperatures, changing weather patterns, fish migration activity, attractants such as animal carcasses floating near shore, and human factors such as increased beach use and heavy fishing. Monitoring shark bite cases globally helps us understand the contributing factors for seasons seemingly high in numbers worldwide.

Historically speaking, 2015 was one of several "summers of the sharks" throughout history. The famous Jersey Shore shark attacks of 1916 became a national concern that led even President Woodrow Wilson to discuss the dangers of sharks with his cabinet. Between July 1 and July 12 of that year, sharks killed four people and severely injured one person. Since then, New Jersey has seen few shark bite cases. Also dubbed the "summer of the sharks," 2001 had its share of high-profile attacks—and some proved fatal. The media was shark-crazy until the terrorist attacks on September 11, 2001; after that, the media and the public lost interest in sharks. Sharks made headlines in 1995, too, until the trial of O. J. Simpson overshadowed them.

The summer of 1980 was a particularly "sharky" summer in the Carolinas. It began in July when a shark knocked a surfer from his board near the fishing pier at Emerald Isle, North Carolina. In the following days, people flooded the local police departments with calls of shark sightings, and fishermen reeled in numerous five-foot sharks off the Iron Steamer Pier in Pine Knoll Shores. In August, marine biologists confirmed that thousands of sharks were swimming in shallow waters from Cape Lookout to Swansboro.[1] This news attracted national media attention, and authorities closed beaches and posted shark warning signs as an extra safety measure. During that year, as in 2015, currents had shifted, moving a surge of very warm water near the strand and drawing fish and sharks closer to the beaches. When a cold front eventually came in, most of the sharks moved away from the shore, and all was back to normal.

Similar to snakes, crocodilians, and predatory cats, sharks fall into the "scary" category for millions of people because of the their ability to injure us as well as their existence in the unfamiliar and unseen underwater environment that we sometimes share. The media—both local and national—feed this fear, manipulating our primal instincts when it comes to sharks by dosing us with story after horror story of shark attacks worldwide and painting a picture of terror, no matter how minor the injury. Even though many more people are killed each year in car wrecks, and even by our canine companions, a shark attack is much more newsworthy, fascinating, and feared.

Shark Attacks in Perspective

So, just how probable *are* your chances of being bitten by a shark when in the water? The truth is that, in comparison with the variety of other accidents that happen to humans worldwide, being bitten by a shark—or, even rarer, death from a shark attack—is statistically trivial. To put things in perspective, think about all the water activities that occur daily, worldwide, year after year, involving millions of people: swimming, wading, boogie boarding, surfing, diving, snorkeling, fishing, skiing, boating, and so forth. Dwell on that image for a moment. Then, compare the following statistics on drowning and shark-related fatalities. According to the United States Lifesaving Association's *National Lifesaving Ocean Drowning Survey,* in 2015 the United States alone recorded 108 ocean drownings; that same year, the Global Shark Attack File documented nine confirmed shark-related fatalities *worldwide.*[2] In 2014, records reported that 114 people drowned in the United States, whereas GSAF records confirmed that sharks had killed only seven people worldwide—and one of those attacks had been a provoked incident. In 2013, drownings of seven people occurred due to rip currents off the coast of North Carolina, making it the fourth most deadly state for swimmers in the United States.[3] That same year in North Carolina, only one person received minor injuries from a shark bite. According to a special report on drowning deaths in North Carolina, 1,052 drownings occurred in the state between 1981 and 1984.[4] During the same period, the Global Shark Attack Database recorded 27 confirmed shark-related fatalities worldwide. So, when it comes to the potential dangers of being in the ocean, the risk of being the victim of a shark attack is very small when compared with the risk of drowning.

Still, no matter how minuscule the chances are of a shark biting a person in the water, the fact remains that any time you enter a marine environment, you face the possibility of a shark encounter. According to Marie Levine, founder of the Shark Research Institute, swimmers, surfers, and other ocean users are likely to be ten to twenty feet from a shark of some species at any point while in the water.[5] In my personal observations made off fishing piers over the years, I have witnessed swimmers completely oblivious to the fact that they were 100 feet or closer to a shark. I have even seen a large shark swim right up to a boogie boarder in waist-deep water. The shark completely ignored the person and continued its search for fish.

Blacktip sharks (henceforth called *blacktips*) and other fish eaters are common in the breakers of the surf zone during summer months in the Carolinas. Airplanes and shark spotters from other parts of the world have reported observing large sharks from deeper water approaching oblivious swimmers and occasionally following them into the shallows before turning away. This means that you are potentially swimming with sharks every time you enter the ocean. Why should this surprise people? Sharks are some of the oldest living animals on the planet. They have been swimming our oceans, estuaries, sounds, and even rivers and lakes for more than 400 million years. Whenever you put yourself in any of these natural bodies of water, you are entering their environment—their home. No one should be surprised that sharks exist in areas where humans choose to swim. The ocean is a wilderness realm—not a backyard swimming pool. Everyone who enters that environment should realize this and respect it. Later in this book, I will share some recommendations for avoiding unwanted encounters—unlikely as they may be.

The Importance of Studying Shark Attacks

I began working with the Shark Research Institute's (SRI) *Global Shark Attack File* (GSAF) in 2004 as a shark bite investigator for North and South Carolina. The GSAF and the Florida-based *International Shark Attack File* (ISAF) are the world's leading sources of facts pertaining to shark attack incidents. In chapter 7, I discuss further details regarding these two organizations as well as specifics on the SRI. During my 14 years of working with the SRI, I have maintained a running database of current and historical records of all shark bite cases and shark–human encounters in the Carolinas. I have actively investigated more than 100 shark-related incidents in both North and South Carolina—and one in Texas. I have communicated and collaborated with globally recognized shark scientists as well as shark bite victims, emergency medical services (EMS) and fire officials, search-and-rescue divers, police officers, military personnel, technical writers, authors, doctors, surgeons, hospital staff, and coroners to gather as much precise data as possible regarding current and historical shark bite incidents and encounters that have occurred in North and South Carolina waters. Crucial reasons for studying shark attacks are that results gathered from investigations help researchers identify shark size and species in attack cases and provide causative factors that may have contributed to an incident. Medical professionals involved in treating shark attack victims also use this information to develop shark bite treatment protocols. Continual contributions to shark bite research allow shark research specialists around the world to establish patterns regarding shark attacks and shark behavior on a global scale.

The study of shark attacks can also help the public better understand how to identify various environmental situations and risk factors, providing a realistic perspective of the actual dangers of encountering a shark. Shark bite investigations and results from these studies—coupled with the media's cooperation in dispersing information and campaigns designed locally to educate beachgoers—can aid researchers in better educating coastal communities on how people can reduce the risk of encountering a shark in the wild. Studying shark attack cases helps provide a safer beach experience for those who use the ocean either recreationally or professionally. Although the likelihood of an attack remains minimal, understanding when the chances of encountering a shark could increase is an extremely important reason to continue research on shark bite cases, and the historical data that shark bite investigators are generating and preserving for the GSAF will greatly benefit generations of people far into the future.

Another major reason for studying shark attacks is to help the public understand a shark's natural predatory behavior and replace the exaggerated fear that people have of these animals with a healthy respect and true appreciation for them and for the vital role that sharks play in our world. After the release of *Jaws,* catching sharks recreationally became a popular sport. The shark hunts of the 1970s contributed to the early decline of shark numbers, but even today, these animals remain increasingly vulnerable to overfishing from the commercial fishing industry as well as from illegal fishing operations, both using massive longline and gill-net fishing methods. Commercial and illegal fishing operations target sharks because of the high demand for shark fins, meat, liver oil, and cartilage. Sharks also become victims of accidental bycatch—primarily from commercial tuna fishing and swordfishing industries. Some studies report that humans kill as many as seventy-three million to one hundred million sharks worldwide each year. Populations of dusky sharks, for example, have declined by more than 80 percent since the 1990s.[6] Sharks are susceptible to longline hooks because, by nature, many species need to remain on the move in search of food and are naturally attracted to fish already trapped by the baited hooks. Swallowed hooks often get stuck in sharks' throats, causing irreparable injuries to vital organs, resulting in starvation and leading to death. Many shark species—including white sharks, basking sharks, and Greenland sharks—are also exceptionally slow breeders, taking many years to reach sexual maturity, and some females birth only one or two pups at a time.

According to the *International Action Plan for Sharks,* initiated by the Convention on International Trade in Endangered Species (CITES) and the Food and Agriculture Organization of the United Nations (FAO), more than 100 of 400 shark species are being commercially exploited. Many of these shark species are so overexploited that we can no longer guarantee their long-term survival. The highly lucrative international shark trade suffers from a serious lack of effective and enforced monitoring and control programs.[7]

Understanding the importance sharks are to us and to the environment and putting the risk of shark bites on humans into a realistic perspective generates appreciation for these animals and highlights their value. When people place a value on something, they are more prone to protect it—and sharks are a crucial animal to protect. Helping to save these animals from the threat of extinction remains the primary reason to continue the study of shark–human relationships and encounters.

Why Do Sharks Sometimes Bite?

Understanding the behavior of sharks, specifically what triggers them to occasionally bite a person, is not an easy thing to do. There is even debate on what exactly a shark attack *is,* and whether such cases should even be called *attacks.* Some researchers claim that all shark attacks should be renamed shark *accidents* for the benefit of the animal. Because most sharks do not target humans as prey, these researchers believe that all such incidents are accidents. Even though I do agree that all shark attacks—ranging from minor injuries to fatalities—are accidents, for the purposes of this book we will continue to consider these incidents as *shark attacks,* and we will define that term simply as a shark biting a person due to a variety of possible motivations, all of which we discuss below. After all, the animal *did* launch an aggressive response to some sort of stimulus from the victim. What is most important in these cases is (1) attempting to determine factors in each incident that may have triggered the shark to attack in the first place and (2) putting forth successful measures to prevent similar incidents from occurring in the future.

There are two basic categories of shark attacks: provoked and unprovoked. *Provoked attacks* are usually defense bites from a shark triggered by provocation, either intentional or unintentional, by the victim. *Intentional provocation* is when a person willingly harasses or places their hands on a shark. Many *intentional provoked attacks* involve fishing activity, as in the following incidents:

On June 29, 2017, a man was bitten on the arm by a juvenile tiger shark that was hooked at Johnnie Mercers Fishing Pier in Wrightsville Beach, North Carolina. Video of the incident shows two men entering the water at the pier to help the animal to shore. One man grabbed the shark by the tail, and the animal reacted by turning around and biting. A pool of blood gushed into the water, and the man left in haste for emergency treatment. Those involved in this incident claim that the man was injured by the fishing hook and not the shark, but the footage suggests otherwise. (Case #GSAF 2017.06.29)

On June 29, 1960, Monte Gray was fishing with Dan Winsett and Ray Allen at Little River Beach in Horry County, South Carolina. At around 2:00 p.m., Winsett hooked a seven-foot shark from the beach. Gray ran into the water to help land the fish. As he stood on a sandbar, the hooked shark bit into his calf. He sustained a seven-inch laceration to his calf and lacerations to his wrist and thumb. (Case #GSAF 1960.06.29)

On September 24, 1960, at Atlantic Beach, South Carolina, Theldon Gore found himself inside a fishing net he had set with an estimated eight-foot, 600-pound shark. Witnesses said that the shark "made a beeline" for Gore, who was churning up the water. Before Gore could get out of the way, the shark clamped down on his left leg. Three men came to Gore's assistance and struck the shark with knives until it released him. The shark broke through the net and swam away. Gore was treated for multiple lacerations in fifteen to twenty places on his left leg, right hand, and arm. (Case #GSAF 1960.09.24)

Professor Frank J. Schwartz of the UNC Institute of Marine Sciences has documented that, in 1983, several commercial fishermen off the North Carolina coast received minor lacerations to their feet from blue sharks during their fishing operations. (Case #GSAF 1983.00.00b)

On January 24, 1983, sixty miles southeast of Beaufort, North Carolina, Chandler Wynn was severely bitten by a shark that got tangled in fishing gear when it was hauled aboard the seventy-one-foot fishing boat, the *Tikki XII*. (Case #GSAF 1983.01.24)

Sometimes people find themselves in a situation where they have placed a shark in a position in which the animal feels threatened, such as invading its personal space or cutting off its swimming path into deeper water, even though the individual(s) may not have known that the shark was even there. These acts are not intentional on the part of the person—they did not intentionally touch the animal or attempt to catch it. In my research I consider these cases to be *unintentional provoked attacks,* as documented in the following Carolina cases:

On August 22, 2007, diver Bruce Pennington received a minor injury to his right hand from a five-foot sand tiger shark as he was conducting an educational program with the North Carolina Aquarium at Fort Fisher in New Hanover County, North Carolina. Pennington was diving in the facility's 235,000-gallon display tank and was in the process of answering questions. When he rotated his hand behind him, it came into contact with the animal, and the shark reacted naturally by biting him. (Case #GSAF 2007.08.22)

In early July 1995, near 29th Avenue, Myrtle Beach, South Carolina, Roberto Perez had his foot bitten by a shark when he jumped off his surfboard in chest-deep water and landed right on top of it. (Case #GSAF 1995.07.00)

In August 2006, Miriam and John Picklesimer were boating off Masonboro Island, about two miles from the inlet, in New Hanover County, North Carolina. The couple had a two-person kayak with them, and at around noon they boarded it to paddle to shore from their anchored skiff. When they reached water about chest-deep, Miriam hopped out of the kayak with a beach bag and chair to wade to shore while her husband planned to paddle back to their boat to get a cooler. As Miriam jumped into the water, which was about 100 feet past a sandbar, a shark hit her on the left foot. She immediately called out to her husband for help. He got her out of the water and drove her to a doctor. She sustained three rows of punctures and lacerations to her left foot. John said that her left heel was hanging off the foot. She received 29 stitches. It seems that Miriam jumped right in front of a passing shark, and it reacted instinctively, likely as a defense mechanism. (Case #GSAF 2006.08.00b)

Unprovoked shark attacks occur when a shark makes the first contact with a human, triggered by some sort of stimulus coming from the victim or the surrounding environment and motivating the shark's attention. These stimuli may include environmental conditions at the scene, any activity in which the victim was engaged prior to the bite, details regarding what the victim had been wearing or any injuries that a victim had sustained prior to the bite, and the time of day during which the bite occurred. Researchers must evaluate all of these criteria to attempt to determine what factors initiated an unprovoked shark attack upon a human being. Through the pioneering and ongoing research of historical and current shark attack data from individuals such as Ralph S. Collier, Dr. A. Peter Klimley, the late Victor M. Coppleson, the late David H. Baldridge, and many others, the shark research community has developed several theories that attempt to explain some of the many reasons that a person might suffer from an unprovoked shark bite. I outline the five most common unprovoked shark attacks below.

Mistaken-identity bites: Mistaken identity is by far the most common reason for a shark biting someone in Carolina waters. When a bite results from mistaken identity, it's usually a case of the animal mistaking some part of a swimmer or surfer for its intended meal. Reasons for a shark to mistake a person for its normal prey include turbid and murky water conditions hindering the shark's vision; baitfish in the area of a swimmer; erratic splashing and movement from a victim that generates sounds similar to those of prey; shiny jewelry such as rings, anklets, necklaces, or toe rings resembling the sheen of a fish; lightly pigmented skin or uneven tanning on a victim; and intensely colored swimwear or brightly colored recreation boards that create vivid contrast in the water, which can imitate the natural colors of a shark's prey. Any one of these situations— or a combination of several—can trigger investigative curiosity and could motivate a shark to bite someone by accident. In the Carolinas, researchers suspect that smaller species such as blacktips and spinner sharks—both swift-moving predators that hunt fish—actually cause these types of injuries. The wounds that these fish eaters leave on human victims are usually minor punctures and lacerations. For example, consider the following incidents:

Chris O'Conner, a sixteen-year-old boy, had been surfing for three hours with some friends on August 12, 2005, in front of Texas Avenue at Carolina Beach, North Carolina. His friends left the water, and Chris stayed out to surf a few more waves. While Chris was surfing, he noticed an unusual amount of minnow-sized fish around him in the water. He also noticed several jellyfish in the area. Chris was preparing to come in for the day, so he caught a wave back to shore. When he got to the shore break, approximately three to five feet from shore, he lost his balance and fell into the water. He was facing seaward underneath the water when he felt something grab his right arm. At first, Chris thought that his surfboard fins had touched his arm, but when he got out of the water, he noticed that he was bleeding pretty badly. He started to walk home, and about halfway there, someone stopped him to ask if he was dizzy. Chris had blood dripping off his fingers. The man who stopped him carried his surfboard on to Chris's house. At home, Chris called his mother, and the man who escorted him home called a lifeguard, who then called New Hanover County EMS. Chris was driven from his home to Alabama Avenue at Carolina Beach, where EMS officials wrapped his arm in bandages. Chris's sister took him to the hospital from there. At the hospital, Chris received four binding strips for his wounds. He sustained an approximate five-inch crescent-shaped wound to the right forearm. The space between the individual tooth marks was three-eighths of an inch at the end of the wound. He sustained a half-inch slash wound to the side of his wrist and two puncture wounds—one above and one below the slash wound. (Case #GSAF 2005.08.12)

On August 6, 2005, fourteen-year-old Michael Lamb was swimming with his friend, Will Coster, in chest-deep water approximately fifty yards from shore off of the Isle of Palms in South Carolina. The pair had been in the water for about an hour when Michael dove under a wave. When he surfaced he began kicking his feet to swim. Suddenly he felt something grab his left foot. At first Michael thought that it was Will grabbing him, so he jerked his foot away. When he did so, though, he felt what he described as a "ripping" sensation. The two boys left the water, and Will went to get an officer who was patrolling the beach. Michael sustained a minor injury to his left foot. There was a cut to the top of the fifth toe at the toenail and a cut to the side of the fifth toe. There were also "V-shaped wounds," one puncturing the knuckle of the same toe, two more above the knuckle, and one puncture wound between the fourth and fifth toe. There were two pieces of flesh missing out of the bottom of the foot—one piece from the bottom of the fifth toe and one piece from the palm of the foot. Michael's wounds required no stitches. (Case #GSAF 2005.08.08)

....

Bites may also result from a mistake in identity by larger, more dangerous shark species such as bull sharks, tiger sharks, and white sharks. These animals are built to hunt large prey at the surface, and an accidental bite from one of these sharks is usually more severe and can even be fatal. I will discuss shark bites from these species in more detail later in the book.

Investigative bites: Inquisitive by nature, sharks often mouth or bite unfamiliar objects in their environment to discover what they are—and to determine whether they are edible. Many of the same factors that result in mistaken-identity bites can, in different circumstances, trigger an *investigative bite* from a shark. Surfers, for example, are sometimes targets for mistaken-identity and investigative bites. Most of the time, when a shark determines that an object it bites is not something that it wants, it will discontinue biting. In cases of investigative bites from large sharks—as with mistaken-identity bites—the damage can result in severe injuries and even death.

....

In July 1907, Mr. C. B. Hernandez was floating on his back in about fifteen feet of water in a small creek behind Coles Island, South Carolina, when a shark appeared and "grabbed hold of" his left knee. The shark immediately bit a second time, getting a better grasp of the lower part of Hernandez's leg. Hernandez managed to fight off the shark and then swam back to the dock. Mr. Charles Millikan was standing at the head of the wharf when the shark attacked Hernandez. Both Millikan and Hernandez clearly saw the shark, which both men agreed was approximately five feet long. The scars on Mr. Hernandez's left leg were crescent-shaped. Investigators did not determine the species of shark involved; however, the behavior of the shark—grabbing the victim's knee and biting a second time before letting go—is consistent with investigative behavior. (Case #GSAF 1907.07.00)

Threat of competition: In certain circumstances a shark may see a human as a competitor for prey. For example, when a swimmer is in the water among a group of baitfish, there is a chance that a shark may see the swimmer as a competitor for food. The following Carolina case may fall under that category:

On Monday, August 21, 2000, along Bogue Banks at Emerald Isle, North Carolina, a man in his forties was swimming away from the beach toward a group of porpoises when he received a severe bite slightly above his wrist, resulting in a near amputation. Because the accident occurred as the victim was swimming, it seems that he was hit simply as he took his next stroke. This case potentially supports a bite due to threat of competition. Sharks, dolphins, and porpoises all feed on the same fish. Their presence in the area indicates that the porpoises were possibly hunting fish, and sharks were probably doing the same thing. The victim put himself in a likely feeding event, where sharks and porpoises were competing for food, and the shark could have bitten the man out of that natural—though mistaken—competition between the species. (Case #GSAF 2000.08.21)

Territorial/Personal space invasion bites and defense bites: In certain cases where a victim is bitten multiple times, sometimes with severe tissue loss, two other types of bites can explain these cases: (1) *territorial/personal space invasion bites* and (2) *defense bites.* Bites that are possibly motivated by one of these theories can prove fatal, yet they are not thought to be the devastating blows of a sneak attack that some species typically deliver to immobilize their prey to feed. Territorial/personal space invasion bites and defense bites can also potentially explain some attacks on boats from white sharks, tiger sharks, bull sharks, and other species. In these cases, the animal might perceive a boat as competition for food, as something invading its territory or personal space, or as something that it must defend itself against—as in the following incident:

On the night of September 26, 1959, Captain E. J. Wines, Major W. Waller, and Major Waller's nine-year-old son, Larry, were in Albergotti Creek—not far from the Marine Corps Air Station Beaufort boat docks in Beaufort, South Carolina—gigging for flounder on a twelve-foot boat. As midnight approached, the trio suddenly became aware of a disturbance in the water caused by a large shark. The shark came at the boat and attacked it, attempting to capsize the vessel. The three individuals quickly headed back for shallow water, poling their craft along the banks for nearly two-and-a-half hours before finally ridding themselves of the shark's assault. The attacking species was recorded as a great white, but species identification is questionable. (Case #GSAF 1959.09.26)

Attacks to feed: As mentioned previously, the majority of shark bites in the Carolinas are from smaller sharks that leave minor lacerations and puncture wounds, but there are cases documented in both North and South Carolina involving a larger animal that actually views a human victim as prey. These attacks are done not out of malice but stem instead from the natural predatory behavior of large animals designed to hunt and kill large prey. Injuries to human victims in these cases are usually quite severe and sometimes result in death. Later in the book, I will cover attacks of this nature.

Major Types of Shark Attacks

According to the ISAF, there are three major categories of shark attacks: hit-and-run attacks, bump-and-bite attacks, and sneak attacks.[8]

Hit-and-run attacks: Hit-and-run shark attacks are the most common type that we see in the Carolinas. They are usually quick in nature and involve only one initial bite—mostly to swimmers, boogie boarders, and surfers within the surf zone. The victim rarely sees the shark. Researchers and investigators believe that most of these types of attacks are cases of mistaken identity by a shark that bites a person's foot, leg, hand, or arm and then quickly lets go after realizing that it has bitten something other than a fish. It then swims off with no further aggression. Victims in these cases are usually left with minor puncture marks and/or slash wounds. These types of attacks usually come from smaller sharks—such as blacktips and spinner sharks—that hunt within the breakers during prime hours when humans are using the water.

Bump-and-bite attacks: Bump-and-bite attacks usually involve larger species of sharks—such as bull sharks and tiger sharks—that hunt bigger prey. These attacks are characterized by a shark circling its victim and bumping into it prior to biting. The shark does this to determine whether its target is of edible interest. These attacks usually result in multiple severe bites that can prove fatal to the victim. Bump-and-bite attacks are rare in the Carolinas, but they *have* occurred.

Sneak attacks: Sneak attacks also involve larger species, such as the white shark. These attacks occur suddenly and without warning. A shark strikes powerfully from beneath, from behind, from the side, or from in front of its target, hitting the victim hard and delivering devastating—in many cases, fatal—injuries. Sneak attacks *have* occurred in the Carolinas, although they are extremely rare.

With both bump-and-bite and sneak attacks, the shark has not mistaken a person for prey; rather, they may actually see the person as their food source. These scenarios do not mean that these animals are "hunting humans"—after all, a shark doesn't even know what a human *is*. What these type of cases *do* mean is that the victims in these circumstances are in the wrong place at the wrong time; in other words, it is possible for a person to be in the water with a large predator that is simply doing what it was designed to do. No matter how rare events such as these are in the Carolinas and worldwide, they still remain a potential risk that we all take when we choose to enter the ocean.

Factors Increasing a Chance Encounter

The chances of encountering a shark while using the ocean are very low; however, the more people there are in the water with more sharks present in a particular area, the likelihood of someone being in the wrong place at the wrong time significally increases. The best tool to provide safety for the public is education. Those who plan to use any marine environment—for pleasure or work—should view the ocean as a vast aquatic wilderness with potential hidden dangers within. Sharks—along with bacteria, rip currents, undertows, jellyfish, and stingrays—are one of those potential dangers. People should not be afraid of the water, but we all must understand that when we enter a marine environment, it is our responsibility to have basic knowledge of our chosen swimming area and to decide if and when it is—or is *not*—a good idea to enter the water. People can reduce their risk of encountering a shark while using the ocean by adhering to the following recommendations.

Never swim, surf, or dive alone: Research has shown that individuals using the water alone are more prone to being bitten by a shark that may be swimming in the area. Being with a companion or a group of people in the water can discourage a shark's curiosity, therefore deterring further investigation. Being with a companion or a group also means more eyes on the water, which provides a greater chance of spotting any impending danger. Finally, if something were to go wrong and you were attacked by a shark or experienced another emergency, having a companion in the water with you allows you to obtain immediate assistance if needed.

Avoid "sharky" areas: Do not swim in areas known to be frequented by sharks or in an area where a shark attack has recently occurred. Leave the water calmly and quietly if sharks are spotted near you. Areas known for being "sharky" are notoriously so for a reason, and common sense should tell you to stay out of the water. For a period of time as determined by local authorities, you should avoid water activities where a shark attack has recently occurred since the same shark or others may still be in the area. If you are in the water and someone has spotted a shark, leave immediately. There could be many sharks close by, and that fact alone greatly increases the risk of injury.

Do not stray too far from shore: Getting yourself into deeper water increases your chances of encountering one of the larger species such as tiger sharks and white sharks. Also, the farther you are from shore, the more distant you are from help should you need it.

Avoid swimming in the late evenings and at night: Studies have shown that sharks move closer to shore in the evenings, and some species are highly active, nocturnal feeders. Many shark bite cases in the Carolinas have occurred in the late afternoon and evening, and some have proved fatal. Swimming at night is a serious risk. Not only are you increasing your chances of encountering a large hunting shark, but you also will not be able to see if there are any potential dangers in the water.

Be careful not to make abrupt movements in the water, and refrain from excess splashing. Do not swim with dogs or other animals: These types of irregular movements in the water from you or a pet could register as an animal in distress to a shark and could attract unwanted attention from a large predator.

Observe the behavior of local wildlife: Avoid swimming in areas where birds are diving into the water, where schools of baitfish are swimming, or where baitfish are leaping above the surface, behaving in an erratic manner, or milling nearby. Also avoid the water if you observe porpoises and dolphins clustering or heading inshore. All of these are indicators of increased chances of sharks in the area. Birds diving indicate that there are schools of fish from which the birds are feeding—and where schools of fish are swimming, usually sharks are present, too. When baitfish leap from the water or swim with jerky, erratic movements, it usually indicates that a predator is after them—that predator could be a shark, or a shark could be attracted to whatever is hunting the baitfish. Your presence could startle milling fish, and sharks find the vibrations of darting, frightened fish very attractive. The presence of porpoises and dolphins may indicate that sharks are hunting in the vicinity. These animals often feed with sharks, and if you observe them clustering and heading shoreward, it could likely have something to do with predatory sharks.

Do not swim near fishing piers: Fishing piers are permanent structures that naturally attract a variety of marine life, including bony fish and sharks. Adding to this natural attractant is the active fishing that occurs on piers most of the year. Shrimp, bloodworms, and squid—as well as fresh-cut fish and live, struggling bait on hooks—attract various species of fish which, in turn, offers constant enticement to sharks. All of this activity continues throughout the day and night. Also, fish-cleaning stations on piers allow discarded entrails back into the ocean, creating somewhat of a chum line at times. This combination of pier structure, fishing activity, and discarded fish parts creates an area that sharks find highly attractive.

Avoid swimming if you are near surf-fishing areas or if fishing boats are close to shore: Areas of high fishing activity indicate that lots of fish are potentially swimming in the vicinity—plus, fishing itself is a process designed to attract fish. In doing so, these areas can also attract sharks looking for an easy meal.

Avoid swimming near natural structures: Sandbars, channels between sandbars, edges of steep drop-offs, jetties, and mouths of rivers and inlets are all areas that attract a variety of marine life. For that reason, these areas can also serve as active feeding sites for sharks.

Avoid high-contrast swimsuits and uneven tanning, and do not swim wearing jewelry: Highly contrasted objects may resemble color variations on fish or may attract investigative curiosity from a predator in the area. A shark can mistake shiny objects such as rings and necklaces for the sheen of a fish.

Do not swim if you have a bleeding cut or an exposed wound: Women should avoid the water if menstruating. Do not urinate in the water while swimming. Human blood and waste in the water can stimulate a shark's senses, thus drawing unwanted attention your way. Menstruation and urination as specific attractants have less scientific support.

Avoid swimming in rough breakers, in turbid water, in murky water, and after heavy rains: Rough, murky water creates a low-visibility situation for you and for any sharks that may be around. Under these circumstances, it is difficult for you to see your surroundings and to determine whether you've placed yourself in a risky situation. It's also more difficult for you to defend yourself against something you cannot see. When in low-visibility situations, a shark could become stressed with the presence of a person, thus increasing the chances of a shark bite. These low-visibility conditions could also trigger an investigative bite from a shark that is simply attempting to find out what you are. In addition, some species —such as the bull shark—prefer to hunt prey in shallow, murky, or turbid areas.

Be aware of changing tides and moon phases: Some studies show that a high percentage of shark bite cases occur during new and full moon phases. The moon's gravitational pull is at its pinnacle during these phases, causing what is known as a *spring tide*. Spring tides occur when each tide is at its highest and lowest points. When spring tide events occur, they affect the movement patterns of various marine organisms, and the food chain moves closer to shore. This, of course, includes sharks.

Ask for advice from local residents or authorities before entering the water: Locals know their local beaches and can give you good advice on where and when not to swim, surf, or dive. Local authorities may have information on any recent shark bites that have occurred in the area, as well.

Pay attention to your instincts: If you are in the water and suddenly become uneasy, get out at once. Certain shark bite case files document the victim having had an unusual feeling of something "not quite right" before their attack. Your instincts are powerful, so you should pay attention to them because they just may be warning you of impending danger. You should also trust your instincts before you enter the water. If you are hesitating or have an unexplained feeling of unease, don't go in.

The above safety recommendations are based on years of research and indicate a higher increase of encountering a shark. The information is universal; however, when using the ocean outside the Carolinas, other advice may be relevant as well (e.g., avoiding swimming, diving, and surfing or kayaking near seal colonies). For additional information on sharks and on shark bite incidents and statistics, visit the SRI and GSAF websites.

3 Shark Attack Statistics for the Carolinas

Sharks have existed on this planet for more than 400 million years and have been responsible for attacks on humans throughout history, with documented incidents dating back as early as ca. 725 B.C. In the United States, North and South Carolina both rank in the top five states for coastlines having the most shark bites, according to a survey that gathered its data from the ISAF and the GSAF.[1]

The following chart lists the total number of confirmed shark attack cases for both North and South Carolina. *Confirmed* indicates that these are undisputed and documented cases of a shark biting a person for some motivated reason. The date ranges are different for North and South Carolina because we intend to show historical, documented shark attack data for our two states (one independent of the other). Researchers have discovered records of attacks in South Carolina dating back as far as 1817, whereas North Carolina's earliest documented case so far occurred in 1853. Since 2004 I have worked with the GSAF by actively investigating shark bites that occur in the Carolinas and searching for historical cases that have not yet been discovered. I source the GSAF with the following information because all of the data has been collected and added through their system.

Confirmed Shark Attacks for North and South Carolina

TYPE OF INJURY	NORTH CAROLINA (1853–2019)	SOUTH CAROLINA (1817–2019)
Non-Fatal (Minor Injuries)	69	129
Non-Fatal (Serious Injuries)	11	8
Fatal Injuries	10	15
Total Number of Attacks	90	152

North and South Carolina Shark Attacks and Fatalities, by Decade

DATE RANGE	CONFIRMED SHARK ATTACKS			FATAL ATTACKS		
	North Carolina	*South Carolina*	*Total, attacks by, date range*	*North Carolina*	*South Carolina*	*Total fatal attacks by date range*
1817–1929	8	17	25	3	5	8
1930–1939	4	4	8	4	0	4
1940–1949	2	15	17	1	10	11
1950–1959	1	4	5	1	0	1
1960–1969	0	6	6	0	0	0
1970–1979	2	3	5	0	0	0
1980–1989	7	14	21	0	0	0
1990–1999	6	16	22	0	0	0
2000–2009	26	28	54	1	0	0
2010–2019	34	45	78	0	0	0
Total, by State	90	152	242	10	15	25

Of the ten confirmed fatal shark attacks in North Carolina from 1853 to 2019, three occurred during a single ship-related incident at sea. In South Carolina, ten of fifteen fatalities from 1817 to 2019 were from a single ship-related incident at sea. Only twenty-five confirmed fatal shark attacks have occurred in both North and South Carolina combined since 1817, and the last confirmed fatal incident occurred in 2001. Historically most shark attack cases in the Carolinas have involved non-fatal injuries (approximately 90 percent in both states). Of the total number of non-fatal attacks resulting in minor injuries, four cases in North Carolina and seven cases in South Carolina were considered provoked incidents, meaning that the shark attacks involved human provocation toward the animal.

These numbers are continually changing in two ways. First, researchers can add numerical data on past shark attack cases to the file for North or South Carolina at any time, as historical cases are newly discovered. Additionally if researchers discover new information about an incident, they can update the data regarding shark involvement. Second, data for new incidents are likely to be added each year. As of the close of 2019, the numbers were continuing to change. North Carolina had five total shark attack cases—one with serious injuries—and zero fatalities for 2019. South Carolina had one shark incident with minor injuries and zero fatalities.

Factors in the Confirmed Cases of Carolina Shark Attacks

The time of day in which most recorded shark attack incidents have occurred in both Carolinas is a reflection of the most common times in which humans use the ocean for recreation. Sharks of various species hunt inshore not only throughout the day but also into the evening, when other species—such as tiger sharks, which may have been patrolling deeper water—also move closer to shore to hunt. The "morning," "afternoon," and "night" sections of figure 1 indicate non-specific timeframes when shark bites have occurred.

In both North and South Carolina, the most common activities— by far—that victims were doing prior to an attack were swimming, wading, or standing in the surf zone, usually in waist-deep water but sometimes in shallower water and at other times in chest-deep water, as shown in figure 2. Incidents involving boogie boards and floats also usually occurred in shallow coastal zone areas. Attacks on surfers usually occurred beyond the breakers into deeper water. It is unknown whether the sounds of humans with flotation items along with the colors of boogie boards, floats, or surfboards invoke additional curiosity from sharks; however, this is certainly a possibility. Historical records show that boating attacks by sharks have included capsized vessels and shipwreck accidents at sea.

In most North and South Carolina shark attacks, the victims sustained minor injuries to their feet, toes, heels, and ankles. In some incidents, two or more bites occurred to two or more body parts (see figure 3).

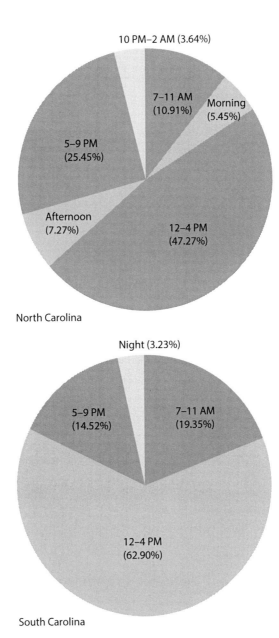

Figure 1. Time of day of shark attacks.

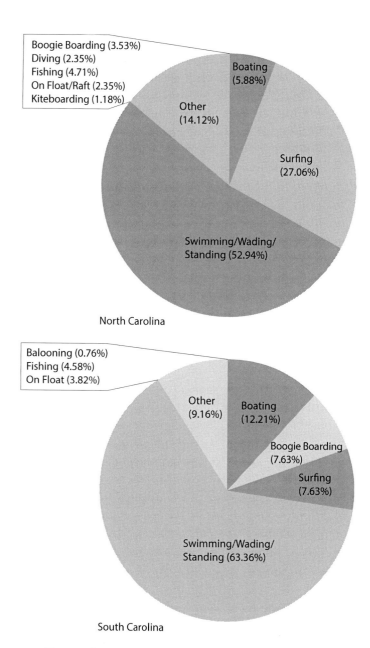

Boogie Boarding (3.53%)
Diving (2.35%)
Fishing (4.71%)
On Float/Raft (2.35%)
Kiteboarding (1.18%)

Boating (5.88%)

Other (14.12%)

Surfing (27.06%)

Swimming/Wading/Standing (52.94%)

North Carolina

Balooning (0.76%)
Fishing (4.58%)
On Float (3.82%)

Other (9.16%)

Boating (12.21%)

Boogie Boarding (7.63%)

Surfing (7.63%)

Swimming/Wading/Standing (63.36%)

South Carolina

Figure 2. Activity victim was engaged in prior to shark attack.

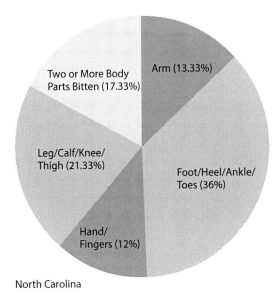

North Carolina

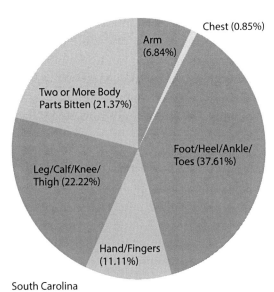

South Carolina

Figure 3. Body parts bitten in non-fatal shark attacks.

Where and When Shark Attacks Occur in the Carolinas

In North Carolina, New Hanover County ranks highest in terms of shark bites, followed by Brunswick, Carteret, and Dare counties. In South Carolina, Charleston County has had the highest number of shark bites, followed by Horry, Beaufort, Georgetown, and Jasper counties (see figure 4).

Of the confirmed North Carolina shark bite cases where researchers were able to record the month, July ranks the highest in shark bite incidents with twenty-eight cases, followed by August with twenty-two cases; February through April show no recorded shark attacks. Of the confirmed South Carolina shark bite cases where researchers were able to record the month, the greatest number of shark bites occurred in July with thirty-four cases, followed closely by June with thirty-two cases. January through March show no recorded shark attacks.

Shark Attack Statistics for the Carolinas, by Month*

MONTH	NORTH CAROLINA (1853–2019)	SOUTH CAROLINA (1817–2019)
January	1	0
February	0	0
March	0	0
April	0	2
May	2	11
June	18	32
July	28	34
August	22	27
September	11	16
October	1	2
November	3	1
December	1	11

Note: Numbers include only cases where the month could be recorded.

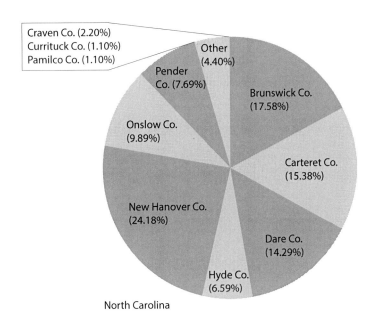

Craven Co. (2.20%)
Currituck Co. (1.10%)
Pamilco Co. (1.10%)

Other (4.40%)

Pender Co. (7.69%)

Brunswick Co. (17.58%)

Onslow Co. (9.89%)

Carteret Co. (15.38%)

New Hanover Co. (24.18%)

Dare Co. (14.29%)

Hyde Co. (6.59%)

North Carolina

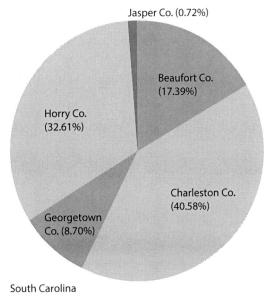

Jasper Co. (0.72%)

Beaufort Co. (17.39%)

Horry Co. (32.61%)

Charleston Co. (40.58%)

Georgetown Co. (8.70%)

South Carolina

Figure 4. Shark attack distribution, by county.

Spikes in Numbers of Bites Explored

It's easy to understand why the summer months have the most shark bite incidents in the Carolinas. When the water begins warming and sustains temperatures in the 70s for longer periods of time, it creates an appealing environment for many species of fish, including several shark species. This is when many seasonal marine visitors arrive in the Carolinas—they are following the preferred warmer waters, the fish migrations, and their own drive to reproduce.[2] The earlier the water warms, the sooner the sharks will arrive in the Carolinas.

This warming of the water also makes the ocean more appealing to humans seeking surf zone recreation. Thus, in the summer months, the Carolinas see the largest number of individuals in the water along with the greatest number of sharks patrolling areas where people swim, making these months prime situations for potential shark–human encounters. Depending on various environmental factors, you will find that some years in the Carolinas have more sharks along the coast than other years—and these natural changes are frequently reflected in the number of shark incidents not only in the Carolinas but worldwide. For example, years with high statistics in North Carolina were 2011 and 2015, each with eight shark attacks; 2010, with five; and 1995, 2006, and 2008, each with six. For the recorded years in between these spikes, North Carolina's shark-incident history ranged from zero to four attacks. When a particular year spikes high in an area, it should be considered part of a normal, global trend.

As regional investigators, we view shark bite incidents on a long-term basis of these high and low spikes to determine whether changes occur from the average number of cases in our given areas. Even with these high and low fluctuations in shark bites per year, you will still see a gradual increase within shark attack data showing higher numbers of shark bites reported in recent years than in the distant past. The easy explanation for this is that higher numbers of people are hitting the beaches as vacation destinations, and humans are logging more hours in the water now than before. In addition, reports of shark bite cases have significantly increased with the aid of advanced communication technology, easy and convenient Internet access, and more interest in the subject from the public. In the past, many bites went unreported or received only local media attention. These days, even a minor shark bite injury gets major news coverage and is in the public eye in a matter of minutes—with the simple click of a button.

Although nothing has changed on a mass scale in terms of shark attack behavior toward humans, some areas show evidence of altered shark migration patterns as a result of human activity. For example, according to an article from the *Bulletin of Marine Science*, "It is thought that the construction and expansion of a large port located just South of Recife, Brazil, has resulted in major environmental degradation and may have displaced bull sharks from their preferred estuarine/inshore habitats to the Jaboatao River and the adjacent lagoon, thus providing an increase of shark and human interactions within the Metropolitan Region of Recife."[3]

In North Carolina, shark researchers Charles Bangley and Roger A. Rulifson conducted a study on environmental conditions associated with the presence of bull sharks in Pamlico Sound and discovered that the sound is now a potential emergent nursery habitat for the species.[4] They documented an increasing trend of juvenile and neonate-sized bull sharks appearing in the sound every year since 2011. This escalation suggests that more bull sharks are being pupped in the Pamlico Sound, making it a potential nursery area for the species. Researchers think that anthropogenic climate change affecting the sound's temperature and salinity is driving this newly discovered pupping behavior.

On a large scale, the fact remains that when warm-water fluctuations and shifts in ocean currents affect migration patterns, bringing fish close to shore, you will also see a corresponding increase in the predators that follow them in closer to our coastlines. These are natural events that were happening long before we chose to use the ocean for recreation.

Details on Carolina Shark Fatalities

The following figures detail fatal shark attacks that have occurred in North and South Carolina waters. The information includes types of injuries that victims received (see figure 5), months where fatal encounters occurred (see figure 6), and activities in which victims were engaged when attacked (see figure 7). Figures 6 and 7 also highlight incidents where authorities did not rule out or confirm a shark attack and did *not* list these incidents as part of the "confirmed" shark bite numbers previously discussed.

The following table lists additional cases and numbers not included in the earlier confirmed shark bite chart and discussion. These cases are important as documented potential additional shark attack incidents; for accuracy, they remain separated from the

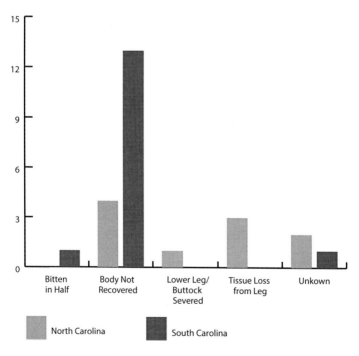

Figure 5. (below) Fatal shark attack injuries.

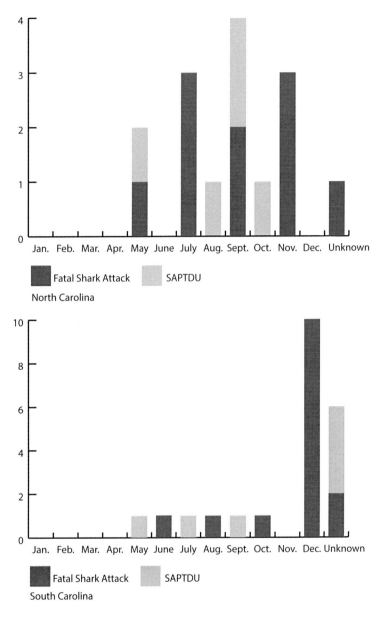

Figure 6. Months in which fatal shark attacks and unconfirmed fatal shark attacks have occurred. (SAPTDU = shark attack prior to death not ruled out or confirmed.)

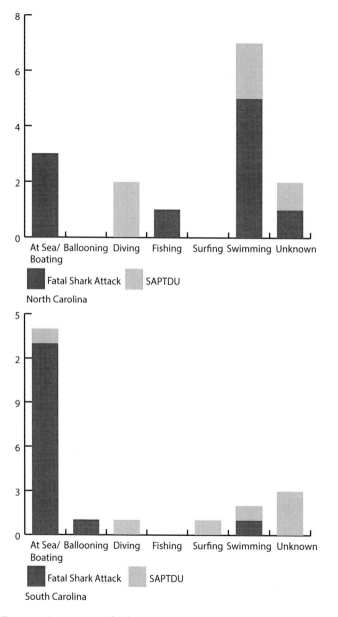

Figure 7. Activity in which victim was engaged prior to fatal shark attack or potentially fatal shark attack. (SAPTDU = shark attack prior to death not ruled out or confirmed.)

actual confirmed number of attacks. Postmortem cases are included here for documentation purposes. They are not considered shark attacks; rather, they are categorized as shark bite incidents that occurred after death. The "confirmed marine animal bite—shark as the attacking species has not been confirmed" category exists primarily because local investigators gave no official word to the media that a shark was involved in a particular case. However, according to surgeon Daniel Segina, MD, shark bite injuries can range from small cuts "to complex wounds," and "sea creature bites are, overall, very uncommon with the overwhelming majority of bites on humans being attributed to sharks." If you think a bite is from a shark, he says, it "almost always" is.[5]

Unconfirmed Shark Attack Statistics and
Postmortem Bite Statistics

TYPE OF INCIDENT	NORTH CAROLINA (1853–2019)	SOUTH CAROLINA (1817–2019)
Shark attack prior to death not ruled out or confirmed	5	7
Questionable incidents	7	8
Confirmed marine animal bite—shark as attacking species not confirmed	8	11
Recorded postmortem cases	1	2

4 Species Involved in Carolina Shark Attacks

Identifying the size and exact species of shark involved in an incident can be difficult, especially if the victim or victim's family is unwilling to assist with an investigation. Without the cooperation of the victim or the family, important details about a case cannot be answered. Investigators and shark experts must then rely on information gathered at the scene: environmental factors; time of day the incident occurred; location of the attack; time of year the incident occurred; depth of water at the attack site; beach conditions; any details about the victim and resulting injuries gathered from witnesses, first responders, doctors, and surgeons; and details from media reports. Knowing many of these specifics, investigators can narrow down the list of potential culprits fairly accurately. In order to attempt a positive identification of a species and the size of the animal involved, local authorities must bring in an expert to view the wounds, or clear and accurate preoperative/pretreatment photos of the wounds must be acquired. While infrequently found during these investigations, if a tooth fragment is recovered, positive identification can usually be obtained

Most shark bite cases in the Carolinas list the attacking species as *unknown*. There are some incidents where media outlets inaccurately report the type of shark involved, and history then records it as gospel. In other cases, even experts cannot agree which species was involved in an attack, and the record becomes documented as either one or the other. Many species in the *Carcharhinidae* family of shark—for example, the blacktip, silky, dusky, spinner, and bull shark—have such similar characteristics that even trained shark bite specialists find it difficult to discern the bite of one species from that of another. It is very likely, especially with historical cases worldwide, that some sharks get more blame than they should for their involvement in attacks, whereas others go unaccused but are true culprits simply not identified correctly.

Of the 500 or so shark species that are identified in the world today, only a handful have been implicated in attacks on humans. Out of that handful, three species stand out far from the rest and are most commonly involved with bump-and-bite attacks and sneak attacks. They are the "apex of the apex predators," a necessary pinnacle in the marine food web. This deadly trio consists of the legendary *great white shark,* the marauding *tiger shark,* and the pugnacious *bull shark.*

Great White Shark
(*Carcharodon carcharias*)

This species is the king of the sharks, the most formidable superpredator of them all, streamlined in shape and massive in build. Ranked third largest of all shark species (behind the whale shark and the basking shark, both plankton feeders), the *white shark*—which is the name preferred by the scientific community—is the largest carnivorous fish alive today. Their heads are wide, tipped with a bullet-shaped snout and framed by a broad set of jaws armed with thick, triangular, heavily serrated upper teeth that can reach up to three inches in length. The lower teeth are also serrated yet narrower than the upper teeth. Although most shark species are cold-blooded, white sharks are partially warm-blooded sharks—endotherms capable of raising their internal temperatures up to 25 degrees Fahrenheit above that of the surrounding seawater, thus allowing them increased rates of neural, digestive, and muscular activities.[1] Their eyes, as black as coal and larger than a softball, lack the nictitating membrane that other species have. Instead, they roll their eyes back for protection from harm when on the attack. Their bodies are slate gray to almost black in color on the dorsal surface; their name is derived from their white to dirty-white underbellies. Swift swimmers, white sharks can burst to speeds of up to 25 miles per hour, sometimes launching themselves completely out of the water during predation. They are inquisitive in nature and are one of the only shark species that practice lifting their heads out of the water to observe the surface world, especially around seal colonies and in circumstances when humans are baiting them to an area. Anyone or anything in the nearby area is subject to investigation from this great predator. White sharks are extremely powerful animals: According to Perry Gilbert—in his book *Sharks and Survival*—there have been documented instances in which a white shark was able to pull apart heavy chain or thick wire rope rated with a breaking strength of 3,800 pounds. On occasion they have also been known to damage and even sink boats.[2]

The white shark's maximum size is debatable. No one really knows how large they can get, but massive ones *do* exist. Ichthyologist John Randall in 1972 conducted a study on bite marks left by white sharks on whale carcasses off the coast of southern Australia and concluded that white sharks of twenty-five to twenty-six feet existed then.[3] In his book, *Shark Man,* shark fisherman Vic Hislop mentions the following:

> I decided to catch the largest great white shark ever and preserve it in a freezer truck to suit my budget. I managed to get four large baits, three stingrays averaging 180 pounds each and a 300-pound greasy cod that a fisherman donated to me. When we reached Phillip Island, Victoria, we were confronted with gale force winds. On the third night of fishing the greasy cod went on the hooks and about 5:30 am we got the strike. The shark grabbed the Queensland cod bait and began pulling the boat backwards. We fought this monster for hours in gale-force winds with twenty-foot-high waves until finally I had it beside us! It was longer than our boat and rounder, and definitely a lot more solid. The shark was 20-feet long and 2.5 tons. . . . There has never, ever been a shark of this enormous bulk caught. But even so I knew it was a baby compared to what is out there.[4]

Other documented giants include a twenty-one-foot white shark (although some disagree with this size) with a reported weight of more than 7,000 pounds caught near the fishing village of Cojimar, Cuba, in 1945; a 20.3-footer caught in 1988 at Prince Edward Island, eastern Canada; and a nineteen-footer found near Ledge Point, western Australia. Shark fisherman Frank Mundus harpooned a seventeen-foot giant in 1964 off Montauk, New York, estimated at 4,500 pounds with a thirteen-foot girth. Shark researchers Scott

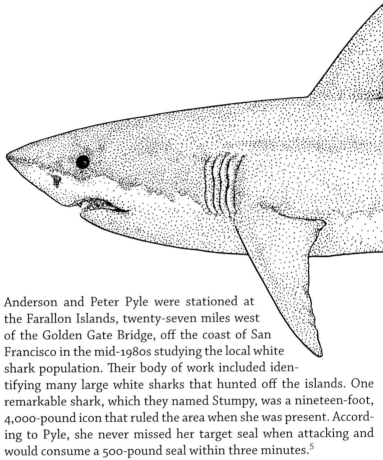

Anderson and Peter Pyle were stationed at the Farallon Islands, twenty-seven miles west of the Golden Gate Bridge, off the coast of San Francisco in the mid-1980s studying the local white shark population. Their body of work included identifying many large white sharks that hunted off the islands. One remarkable shark, which they named Stumpy, was a nineteen-foot, 4,000-pound icon that ruled the area when she was present. According to Pyle, she never missed her target seal when attacking and would consume a 500-pound seal within three minutes.[5]

Perhaps the greatest examples of white sharks' potential size and power come from the incredible experiences that Craig Anthony Ferreira and his father, Theo Ferreira, have had with a legendary shark known as "the Submarine" that roamed the waters of False Bay, South Africa. This giant was known to boldly approach fishing boats, bumping them and scaring fishermen half to death. Some controversy and doubt surround the existence and size of this shark, and Discovery Channel has even fueled that doubt by using the Submarine's name to make sensational false documentaries (for which they received viewer complaints). I personally contacted Craig years

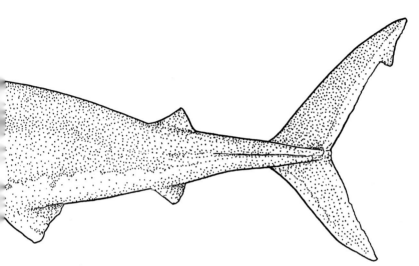

ago with questions on the validity of this animal, and he was ada-mant regarding its reality and magnificence. Today Craig is a special-ist in white sharks and an authority on their behavior. He has led three international white shark exploration projects and has written the first scientific paper regarding the size and age composition of white shark populations in southern Africa. During his many years of working with these animals, Craig has seen many large ones—including several white sharks more than nineteen feet long. He at-tests that the Submarine dwarfed even these massive white sharks. He has described "the Sub" as being at least twenty-three feet long, with such a massive girth that his estimate of the animal's weight was around 11,000 pounds.[6] Craig described her head alone as being almost as wide as the stern of his father's boat, which was eighteen feet long and six feet wide. The men know that this shark was longer than the boat because they witnessed the animal swimming parallel to them alongside the vessel, and its head and tail extended past the bow and stern. Craig often fished with his father at the time of their encounters with the Sub. Theo was an avid shark hunter and was ob-sessed with catching the giant beast. They experienced at least three encounters with the Sub—each time, the shark got away.

Only recently has the general public noticed white sharks roaming Carolina waters. Although this species has always been there with documented sightings, ranging from January to December in the Carolinas, it was the now famous Mary Lee that brought white sharks true attention. Mary Lee is a sixteen-foot-long, 3,500-pound white shark tagged in 2012 off Cape Cod, Massachusetts, by the crew of the Ocearch shark tagging program.[7] Since her tagging, shark experts have learned that she seems to call the East Coast of the United States her home and has routinely traveled up and down the coast from Cape Cod, Massachusetts, to Savannah, Georgia. In the Carolinas, she has surfaced all along the coastal zone—sometimes nearly in the breakers—from Corolla, North Carolina, to Hilton Head Island, South Carolina, and has even ventured into North Carolina's Albemarle Sound and Cape Fear River. These satellite transmissions can be less than optimal if the shark does not remain at the surface long enough for a good location fix. For this reason, these tags can have considerable margins of error. In any case, Mary Lee is a visible testimony of white shark activity within the Carolinas. Aside from Mary Lee, the following incidents serve as additional accounts of the white sharks' presence in the Carolinas:

> One of the earliest reports of a Carolina white shark occurred in May of 1888, when Captain Lorenzo Willis and two boat crews killed a huge shark off Wreck Point near Beaufort, North Carolina. The crew harpooned the shark and fought it for two hours. The shark measured eighteen feet long and eight feet wide from pectoral fin to pectoral fin and weighed two tons. In its stomach researchers found six sharks, the smallest measuring six feet long. The shark's mouth was wide enough to roll a kerosene barrel into it with space to spare. Its teeth were an inch wide and two inches long.[8]

> Shark scientist Russell J. Coles tells of an experience he had with a twenty-foot-plus white shark in 1905. According to Coles, he was harpooning turtles from a small skiff when the shark appeared close enough for him to have reached out and touched it. It hit the side of the skiff with force before seizing a large sea turtle that had surfaced near the skiff. It grabbed

the turtle with its massive jaws and took it beneath the water. Coles also documented his June 1918 observations of a large white shark that he studied in a net off Cape Lookout, North Carolina. He measured the shark and stated that the animal measured twenty-two feet long and weighed two tons. Its head was larger than a fifty-gallon barrel, and its mouth was three feet wide. The shark was eighteen feet in girth at the armpit of the pectorals.[9]

A large white shark was entangled in a longline set by a commercial fishing vessel on September 25, 1984, when Lloyd Davidson, Jon Dodrill, and Sylvester Karasinski were longlining for sharks. This white shark had swallowed a hooked 6-foot tiger shark whole; it had one hook in its stomach, one hook in its mouth, and its tail was wrapped in the cable's bottom mainline. The shark was 15 feet 10 inches long and weighed 2,080 pounds.[10]

In January 2004, Mark Beasenburg and his friend, Danny Nixon, were out on a twenty-four-foot Boston Whaler, ten miles beyond the Charleston Jetties in South Carolina, when they spotted two fins about fourteen feet apart. The men thought that they were viewing two sunfish—until they got closer and discovered that it was a massive white shark about twenty-three feet long. Beasenburg said the shark's diamond-shaped head was about six feet wide—wider than his boat's two twin Johnson 150 HP engines.[11]

On May 13, 2004, Captains Charles Perry and Devon Cage were heading toward Cape Hatteras, looking for cobia (a species of fish), when they came across a white shark nearly eighteen feet in length. They estimated the size of the shark when it swam parallel with the stern of their boat, which was more than fifteen feet wide.[12]

On November 11, 2009, fishermen Steve Boehling and Mike Ross photographed a large white shark about a mile off Wrightsville Beach, New Hanover County, North Carolina.

The two were fishing when the shark appeared. They pulled their eighteen-foot boat alongside the animal and noticed that it was a foot or two shorter than the boat. They described the shark as having very sizable teeth with a solid dorsal surface color, no markings, and a white underbelly. They submitted their photos to Hap Fatzinger, the North Carolina Fort Fisher Aquarium curator, and he confirmed it as looking like a great white.[13]

....

Several more sightings, encounters, and catches of great whites have occurred in the Carolinas, including the following:

April and May 1950: Several white sharks were taken by trawlers off Cape Romain, South Carolina, and in April 1950 a twelve-and-a-half-foot white shark was landed.[14]

April 1974: Juvenile white shark caught on a longline set off of Shackleford Banks between Cape Lookout and Beaufort Inlet, North Carolina.[16]

July 1983: A small white shark measuring 4'5½" long was landed by a surf fisherman on the western end of Onslow Beach, Onslow County, North Carolina.

1984: A white shark was landed off Cape Romain, South Carolina.

December 13, 1984: A 4'8¼" white shark was landed near the shipwreck *Papoose* near Cape Lookout, North Carolina.

April 27, 1985: A young female white shark measuring longer than seven feet and weighing 250 pounds was landed two miles off Wrightsville Beach—one mile north of the Wrightsville Jetty, North Carolina.

March 29, 1986: A twelve-foot white shark was caught in Bogue Inlet, North Carolina.

April 1986: A fifteen-foot white shark weighing 2,143 pounds was landed twenty miles offshore of Beaufort Inlet, North Carolina.[17]

July 11, 1987: In Winyah Bay between Charleston and Myrtle Beach, South Carolina, a twelve-foot white shark grabbed the descending anchor of the DeMaurice family's seventeen-foot fishing boat, pulling the front of the boat beneath the surface briefly and towing them until the anchor line was cut.[18] (Case #GSAF 1987.07.11)

1988: A fisherman claimed that he saw a massive white shark, twenty-six feet long, twenty miles off Emerald Isle, North Carolina.

Summer 1988: A fisherman reported seeing a twenty-five-foot to thirty-foot white shark in the main channel of the Cape Fear River between Bald Head Island and Southport, North Carolina.

April 26, 1989: A fifteen-foot female white shark weighing 1,231.1 pounds with a forty-inch girth was caught several miles off Bulls Bay, South Carolina, in twenty-one fathoms of water.

May 1989: A seven-foot white shark was landed just off the entrance to Charleston Harbor, South Carolina.

Spring 1989: A large white shark was spotted in an area two hundred yards off the Isle of Palms, South Carolina.[19]

July 1993: A juvenile white shark weighing twenty-nine pounds was discovered tangled in longlines about fifty miles off Charleston, South Carolina.[20]

December 15, 1995: A seven-foot young male white shark was hooked about five miles off Folly Beach, South Carolina.[21]

January 1996: Juvenile white shark landed about twenty miles south of Cape Lookout, North Carolina.

May 3, 1996: Two large white sharks were caught at Ocracoke, North Carolina; three white shark pups washed ashore that same month.

May 18, 1996: Two people aboard a ten-foot boat spotted a white shark estimated to be twenty feet long just off Wrightsville Beach, North Carolina.

May 1996: Two juvenile white sharks were landed off Core Banks, North Carolina.

December 12, 1998: A fourteen-foot seven-inch white shark with a nine-foot girth around the pectoral fins was found floating dead in the Intracoastal Waterway near Wilmington, North Carolina.[22]

December 12, 1998: A female white shark estimated at 900 pounds washed up on the beach near Carolina Beach, North Carolina. Coast guard personnel took photos of the shark.[23]

August 5, 2000: A large white shark was spotted at the site of the sunken tanker, the *Atlas,* fifteen miles east of Cape Lookout, North Carolina.[24]

July 21, 2001: A white shark was spotted at the *Caribsea* wreck site, located five miles north of the *Atlas* (a sunken tanker) off Cape Lookout, North Carolina.[25]

April 2008: A large white shark was spotted near the shipwreck *Vermillion,* located southeast of Murrells Inlet, South Carolina.[26]

May 3, 2008: A ten-foot female white shark was caught approximately five miles off Garden City, South Carolina.

November 18, 2008: A thirteen-foot two-inch white shark was discovered stranded on the beach near the Morris Island lighthouse in Folly Beach, South Carolina.

November 19, 2011: Twenty-five miles southeast of Wrightsville Beach, North Carolina, an eighteen-foot white shark nudged and tail-slapped a fishing boat.[27]

December 7, 2015: A white shark measuring eight feet and weighing approximately 500 pounds washed ashore around noon next to Crystal Pier at Wrightsville Beach, North Carolina.[28]

March 22, 2016: Coast Guard Crew members from U.S. Coast Guard Station Fort Macon photographed an estimated eighteen-foot white shark eating a juvenile twelve- to fourteen-foot minke whale about eight miles south of Beaufort Inlet, North Carolina.[29]

February 1, 2017: Chip Michelove and crew were tagging sharks sixteen miles off Hilton Head Island, South Carolina, when a fourteen-foot white shark bit their boat.[30]

March 17, 2017: Jannick Schroder and two friends were fishing thirty miles offshore of Wrightsville Beach, North Carolina, at 23-Mile Rock when a ten- to twelve-foot white shark appeared and bit a hooked sandbar shark in half (the sandbar shark weighed 140 to 180 pounds). The white shark then rammed the boat and bit the motor, knocking the passengers off their feet.[31]

April 1, 2017: About one-and-a-half miles east of the Oceanana Pier, Atlantic Beach, North Carolina, an eight- to nine-foot white shark came up behind Dan Jendro's boat as he and his friend were preparing to raise the anchor. The shark circled and investigated the boat for about five minutes, running into it a few times and biting the outboard motor before leaving.[32]

The white shark bears the title of "the most dangerous of all sharks." It has been implicated in more attacks on humans that any other species and is accused of causing greater numbers of fatalities than tiger or bull sharks. It is surprising, however—given the size potential of these animals and their powerful ability to kill a person—that a good portion of people who have been attacked by white sharks actually survive their encounters.

As mentioned previously several theories explain a shark's potential motivations for biting a human, but white sharks are one of the few species that, for unknown reasons, do—on very rare occasions—attack and consume people. Perhaps they mistake a person for a preferred food source and follow through with the kill, mistake or not. Maybe the shark hasn't fed for a long period of time and means to kill and consume anything that it finds. Or perhaps the shark recognizes the object (i.e., the human) that it sees and chooses to attack, kill, and consume that "object." Attacks of this nature are usually violent sneak attacks with the shark hitting hard and without warning—sometimes consuming their victim quickly, biting them in half, or leaving a devastating fatal wound, and then swimming away to wait for the prey to die before consuming it. Whatever the reason, white sharks are usually the species that launch attacks of this kind, making them the most dangerous shark in the world.

Documented cases of fatal sneak attacks have occurred in both North and South Carolina, and each one leaves little doubt that a white shark was involved.

....

The earliest account of a Carolina-based sneak attack occurred —on June 24, 1817—and was reported the following day by *The Times* in Charleston, South Carolina. On the day of the attack, an elderly African American man named Jemmy was swimming out to his boat that had set adrift off James Island, near Fort Johnson, located within Charleston Harbor, South Carolina. Just as he reached the boat, a large shark struck him with enough force to have supposedly sliced him in two. The shark disappeared, along with the unfortunate fisherman, who was never seen again. (Case #GSAF 1817.06.24)

Another incident occurred sometime in 1840, when a pilot boat was coming in to dock at its wharf in Charleston Harbor, South Carolina. During the process of lowering the boat's sail, one of the crew members was accidentally thrown overboard. Two other men immediately went to his rescue. As the rescuers were pulling a skiff to the overboard man, a large shark passed by them and headed directly toward the crewman treading water. The shark grabbed the victim and took him underneath the water. A streak of blood circled the spot where the man had been taken. He was never seen again. The shark involved was said to have been twenty-five feet in length. (Case #GSAF 1840.07.22 R)

In 1852, Charles Chambers and a friend were boating near Mount Pleasant, South Carolina, when their boat capsized. Both men took an oar and proceeded to wade into shore. The friend was ahead of Charles when suddenly he looked back and saw Charles attempting to fight off a shark. The friend witnessed Charles being pulled under the water with force, never to be seen again. (Case #GSAF 1852.00.00)

On the afternoon of July 29, 1905, sixteen-year-old Sutton Davis was enjoying the day in the waist-deep water of Core Sound at the Davis Shore near Davis, North Carolina, about ten miles east of Beaufort, North Carolina. As the boy was wading, a large shark suddenly and violently struck him. The shark threw the boy into the air, grabbed him as he hit the water, pulled him under, and swam away with him. Those on shore watched in helpless horror—they could do absolutely nothing to help the young teenager. Investigators conducted a thorough search of the area but found no trace of Sutton. Newspapers of the time reported that people had observed many sharks for two weeks prior to the attack. The media also reported that a large number of menhaden (a species of fish) had been caught during the month of July and a good portion of refuse fat from these fish had been thrown back into the water from nearby factories. This refuse fat likely attracted sharks to the area to feast, and some people believed that it was a causative factor contributing to Sutton Davis's tragic death. (Case #GSAF 1905.07.29)

On October 26, 1911, the steamship *Rio Grande* was traveling to New York from Brunswick, Georgia. On this date, while the ship was off the coast of Charleston, South Carolina, sailor George Spencer fell overboard and was bitten in two by a large shark. Several of the ship's passengers witnessed Mr. Spencer's struggle with the fish, which quickly took him beneath the surface and disappeared. (Case #GSAF 1911.10.26)

Although experts have not scientifically confirmed any of the above cases as white shark attacks, as an investigator I believe it's fairly safe to say that the species was likely involved in all of the incidents. Each fatality discussed above exactly fits the pattern of a white shark consuming a human victim as prey. To underscore my point, I have included the following fatal and confirmed white shark sneak attacks that have occurred in other parts of the United States and throughout the world. Notice their close similarities with the Carolina cases previously covered.

On February 8, 2014, a large white shark consumed twenty-eight-year-old Sam Kellet while he was spearfishing with a group of friends in the Gulf of St. Vincent off Goldsmith Beach on the Yorke Peninsula, South Australia. Witnesses described seeing a large white shark thrash its tail and launch itself out of the water. They did not see the victim being attacked, but there was a large pool of blood where Kellet was last seen. One witness stated that he looked underwater and saw a large shark in the exact position where he had last seen Kellet. He said that the shark was thrashing in a vertical position with its head facing the surface and its tail toward the seafloor. Local authorities never found Kellet's body, but police divers found his spear gun and two lead weights. The spear gun had serrated incisions on it that were compatible with a white shark's tooth impressions.[33] (Case #GSAF 2014.02.08)

On January 12, 2010, a shark killed and consumed thirty-year-old Lloyd Skinner. Witnesses described the shark as being longer than a minibus. Skinner was in the ocean off Fish Hoek Beach in Cape Town, South Africa. He was standing in chest-deep water adjusting his goggles when a shark hit him with a massive strike. The shark then circled and hit him again, knocking him into the air before pulling him beneath the water, never to be seen again. (Case #GSAF 2010.01.12)

On September 25, 2000, 17-year-old Jevan Wright was surfing at Blacks Point, near Elliston, South Australia, when a huge shark appeared, grabbing both surfer and board in its mouth. The shark attacked from behind, and witnesses said that the board was broken in half but that there seemed to be no struggle and no visible signs of blood in the water. Jevan was just gone, never to be seen again. (Case #GSAF 2000.09.25)

On September 24, 2000, Cameron Bayes was surfing alone at Cactus Beach, near Penong, South Australia, when a white shark hit his surfboard, knocking Bayes into the water. He managed to climb back onto his board and was paddling back to shore when the shark struck again, biting the surfboard in half and taking Bayes underwater. He was never seen again. (Case #GSAF 2000.09.24)

On March 3, 1985, 33-year-old Shirley Ann Durdin, her husband Barry Durdin, and friend, Keith Coventry, were swimming back to shore at Wiseman's Beach, located in Peake Bay, South Australia. The three had been snorkeling and diving for scallops and were on their way to rejoin their friends and family who were on the beach. Shirley was in water about seven feet deep when she was violently struck by a huge white shark that witnesses estimated was nearly twenty feet long. With the first strike, the shark severed both of her legs. Barry was standing on a submerged rock a little more than 30 feet from her when he heard her yell out. Keith turned around when he heard her scream and saw Shirley suspended high above the water as the shark's huge fin broke the surface. He noticed some thrashing and the water turning dark around her. Realizing that she was gone, Keith kept Barry from swimming to her, fearing for Barry's safety. Nearby boats rushed to the area to give what assistance they could, but when they arrived, the shark had removed the victim's head and one arm. Ignoring the boats, the shark circled the remains and took them, retreating toward the deep water of the bay. Local fishermen reported that a large white shark had been seen in the area for a month prior to the attack. Investigators believe that the shark was attracted to the area by offal that a resident fishing company had thrown into the water at Wiseman's Beach. (Case #GSAF 1985.03.03)

On June 14, 1959, thirty-three-year-old Robert Pamperin and companion Gerald Lehrer were diving for abalone off the west end of La Jolla Cove in California when a large white shark consumed Pamperin. The divers had been more than one hundred feet from shore and had drifted apart while collecting their catch when Pamperin suddenly started thrashing in a panic and shouted for help. Hearing the panic call, Lehrer rapidly swam to his friend. He witnessed his friend slowly vanish from the water's surface, which was now red with Pamperin's blood. Lehrer dove beneath the water and, in horror, saw his friend, waist-deep in the shark's jaws. After gasping for another breath, Lehrer submerged twice more to try and help his companion. He saw the shark lying nearly upside down on the bottom, shaking its head from side to side, so Lehrer tried in vain to scare the beast, hoping that it would release Pamperin. He soon realized that there was absolutely nothing he could do to save his friend, so he swam back to shore for help. No trace of Robert Pamperin's body was ever found. (Case #GSAF 1959.06.14)

On February 11, 1950, fourteen-year-old Clive Dumayne and four friends were body surfing at South Beach, Durban,

KwaZulu, South Africa, when a white shark estimated at around 12 feet long surfaced between Dumayne and his friends. The shark passed the friends and went for Dumayne, who was closest to shore. The shark emerged from the water, hit the young boy, and took him under. Dumayne reappeared at the surface briefly, screamed, and was pulled under the surface for the last time. No trace of him was ever found. (Case #GSAF.1950.02.11)

On Tuesday, February 4, 1936, more than 100 people were in the surf at South Steyne on the southern end of Manly Beach, New South Wales, Australia. Fourteen-year-old David Paton and several other swimmers were farther out than the rest. Around 3:00 p.m., onlookers witnessed a huge dark shape surface from beneath the water and slam down on Paton. Don Redington and beach inspector Dudley Beer immediately went to the spot where the boy disappeared but could not find a single trace of him. Paton was never seen again. Witnesses claim that they saw what looked like a white shark cruising near a bank of seaweed close to the beach. (Case #GSAF 1936.02.04)

On Wednesday, January 22, 1936, at around 6:00 p.m., thirteen-year-old Ray Bennett, a newspaper boy who had completed his day's sales, entered the ocean to cool off at West Beach, near Adelaide, South Australia. Bennett was only sixty to sixty-five feet from shore in waist-deep water when a large shark breached the water and quickly disappeared with Bennett, leaving only a patch of foam sitting on the surface of the water where the swimmer had been only moments before. Bennett's fourteen-year-old sister witnessed the attack, and she quickly ran to the spot where it had occurred but could not find her brother. Len Bedford, an eighteen-year-old boy on the beach, stated that he heard a scream from the water. He saw a swimmer struggling, and then he watched the shark come out of the water, its tail sticking up in the air where the bather had vanished. Ray Bennett was never seen again.

Historical accounts report that a large white shark was responsible for his death. (Case #GSAF 1936.01.22)

....

In the Carolinas, two shark attacks on record—one in North Carolina and the other in South Carolina—implicate a white shark as the attacking species. Official reports from that time reveal little information as to how investigators concluded that a white shark was involved in either case. Therefore, other large species should be considered as possible suspects; however, a white shark cannot be ruled out as the attacking species due to the severity of the injuries.

....

On July 15, 1957, fifty-seven-year-old Rupert Wade was a resident of Morehead City, North Carolina, and was a well-known long-distance swimmer who often swam far from shore. Wade was swimming with his lifeguard friend Billy Shaw at Salter Path in Atlantic beach, North Carolina. The two of them were in the water for about fifteen minutes and were more than 1,000 feet from shore when Wade suddenly yelled to Shaw that a shark had attacked him. Shaw swam to his friend to assist, but Wade told him to swim to shore for help. He did so and notified the Coast Guard. When they arrived at the spot where Shaw had last seen his friend, they found Wade floating at the surface. They retrieved him and took him to the Coast Guard station where an ambulance awaited, ready to transport him to Morehead City Hospital (now Carteret Health Care Medical Center). EMS workers administered artificial respiration en route but could not revive him. Wade was pronounced dead at the hospital. He had received a massive bite to his right leg midway between his hip and knee. The wounds were deep enough to expose the bone. He also suffered deep cuts on his right foot. Investigators attributed Wade's death to a white shark. Wade had been a great distance from shore, thus increasing his chances of encountering a shark, and the specifics of his attack are similar to those in other white shark incidents—and possibly were not motivated by feeding. However, a bull shark or tiger shark could have been involved in this incident. (Case #GSAF 1957.07.15)

On August 16, 1961, nineteen-year-old Camden Military Academy student William Lee Baily was enjoying a sunny morning in the ocean at Pawleys Island, South Carolina. At approximately 8:00 a.m., he was swimming about fifty feet from shore in around six feet of water when he was attacked by what eyewitness Paul Q. Quinn described as a white shark. The shark tore into Baily's right arm and severely mangled his left leg. Baily was taken to Georgetown Memorial Hospital, where he received approximately 163 stitches to close the wound to his arm. His left leg required amputation the following day due to the severity of the wound. The ISAF records this incident as a white shark attack, as does the GSAF. A bull shark or tiger shark could also have been the species involved in this incident. (Case #GSAF 1961.08.16)

As mentioned, a good portion of people who are attacked by white sharks actually survive their encounters. Worldwide, most white shark attacks are non-fatal, likely because most of these encounters are investigative in nature or are motivated by some other reason unrelated to predation. As shown earlier, the statistics for fatal attacks by white sharks in both North and South Carolina remain low.

Tiger Shark
(*Galeocerdo cuvier*)

Tarpon, moray eels, gray mullet, sole, sharks, sea turtles, sea lions, seals, dolphins, stingrays, sea snakes, iguanas, crocodiles, frigate birds, cormorants, pelicans, penguins, albatross, whale meat, crayfish, crabs, octopuses, chickens, rats, pigs, sheep, dogs, hyenas, monkeys, a porcupine, songbirds, a bag of money, leather coats, boat cushions, driftwood, conch shells, a large tom-tom drum, horseshoe crabs, an unopened can of salmon, a wallet, a two-pound coil of copper wire, nuts and bolts, bundles of wool, cotton, silk, pens, plastic bags, rubber tires, cans, bottles, pieces of metal, bags of potatoes, coal, a driver's license, a cow's hoof, a horse's skull, a deer's antlers, lobsters, a chicken coop with feathers and bones inside, license plates, gasoline cans, cigarette tins, men, women, and children all have been found in the stomachs of tiger sharks at one time or another, making them the least specialized species when it comes to diet. These sharks are both predators and scavengers, and they will eat anything that crosses their paths. Because of this nonselective behavior, they have earned the well-deserved nickname—the "garbage cans of the sea."

Tigers are one of the largest shark species in terms of total size, falling under only three other species: the white shark, the basking shark, and the whale shark. They can reach a length of twenty feet and weigh more than one ton. Historical data report even larger tiger sharks. In 1957, someone caught a female tiger shark off the coast of Indo-China. Reports from the time estimated that it was twenty-four feet long and weighed 6,856 pounds. Both Carolinas have recorded large catches of this species, including the following accounts: Walter Maxwell's world-record 1,780-pound tiger shark from Cherry Grove Pier in South Carolina; Maxwell's North Carolina state-record 1,150-pound tiger shark catch off the Yaupon Pier on Oak Island, North Carolina; a twelve-foot 1,200-pound tiger shark caught eight miles offshore at Little River, South Carolina[34]; and an eleven-footer that someone landed about five miles east of Wrightsville Beach, North Carolina.[35]

These predators vary in color from brown, black, gray, or olive on the dorsal (back) surface to a yellowish, white, or light-gray color on the ventral (belly) surface. Young tiger sharks have dark vertical stripes or blotchlike markings along their bodies that fade with age and that are often absent altogether in adults. They are stoutly built yet have a streamlined appearance. A tiger shark's head is flattened and very broad, with a characteristically short and rounded snout. Their eyes are large and jet-black, with a nictitating membrane that shields them when instinct dictates.

Tiger sharks have unique, broad, triangular-shaped cutting teeth that are strongly serrated and notched at the outer margins. Unlike those of most sharks, the teeth of a tiger shark are similar in both the upper and lower jaws. These curve-angled teeth are firmly placed within a set of somewhat squared jaws, are thickly calcified, and are attached to musculature powerful enough to bite clean through a sea turtle's shell. This combination of jaw power and unique sawlike

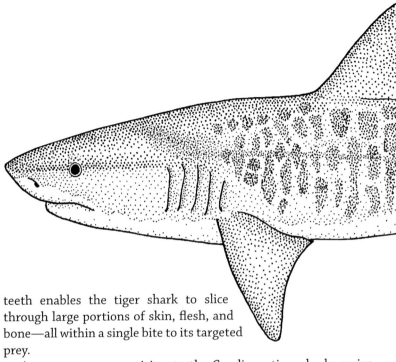

teeth enables the tiger shark to slice through large portions of skin, flesh, and bone—all within a single bite to its targeted prey.

A common summer visitor to the Carolinas, tiger sharks arrive inshore as early as April and may linger near the coast until as late as November. They are also found offshore of the Carolinas year-round. During their inshore prowls, they hunt the surf zone, getting closer to shore as the sun sets. They also enter sounds, inlets, and saltwater sections of large rivers. In May 2015, the research organization Ocearch tagged a twelve-foot, 1,200-pound tiger shark dubbed "Chessie" off the coast of South Carolina.[36] On the morning of June 11, 2015, at 3:30 a.m., she surfaced in the Cape Fear River near Fort Fisher, North Carolina. She was likely hunting for food, given the common nocturnal hunting habits of tiger sharks.

In the Carolinas, incidents involving tiger sharks have been recorded, but in most cases, the species involved is actually not confirmed. Tiger sharks are, however, likely to have been involved in more incidents where the record lists the attacking species as "unidentified"—especially in some of the cases involving serious

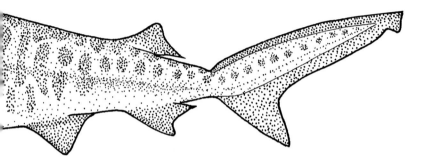

injuries and fatalities. Because of their potential proximity to swimmers, their large size, their tendency to be curious, and their indiscriminate eating habits, the tiger shark is one of the most dangerous sharks, second only to the white shark in terms of attacks on humans and is known to be persistent when pursuing a meal. Researchers have discovered that it has executed multiple attacks—at times, on the same day.

Historical data shows that the earliest recorded Carolina tiger incident happened on July 13, 1853, when a large tiger shark surfaced and launched itself at a group of men bathing in Charleston Harbor, where they had anchored their ship. A shipmate on board warned the men, who immediately swam toward the vessel for safety. All but one made it aboard. Witnesses said that the shark bit the victim in two. A friend entered the water with a knife and killed the animal. The remains of the victim were recovered from the shark's stomach, where they were buried with the rest of the body. The shark was reported to have been a large female tiger shark that gave birth to twenty-two pups after being retrieved. An additional twenty-one pups were said to have been found inside of her once she was cut open. This case is considered a "questionable incident" because of its similarity to another attack that reportedly took place in Barbados. (Case #GSAF 1853.07.13)

The remains of a young woman between the ages of twenty-eight and thirty-eight were recovered from the stomach of an eight-foot tiger shark in May 1982. The tiger shark was landed by a fisherman in Port Royal, South Carolina, who was fishing off Daws Island in the Broad River near Beaufort, South Carolina. The fisherman had sold the shark to a buyer and was waiting for the purchaser to arrive. While waiting, he began examining the stomach contents of his catch and noticed a suspicious-looking bone among the contents. In all, the shark's stomach contained the proximal fourth of a left tibia and fibula, a complete patella, and two distal fragments of a femur bone. The coroner who examined the remains speculated that the bones could have been those of a passenger from a recent plane crash that had occurred in the area, considering not all bodies of that accident had been recovered; however, investigators could not determine an official cause of death in this case. (Case #GSAF 1982.05.00)

On July 19, 1985, what was thought to have been an eight- to nine-foot tiger shark suddenly attacked ten-year-old Julie Steed. She was playing with her father in the surf at Folly Island, Charleston, South Carolina, when she was severely bitten. They had a two-person raft with them for riding waves, and they were returning to shore when the shark grabbed her leg. Julie said that although the attack was a total surprise, she remained calm. Her father, David Steed, came to her rescue and held on to his daughter. The shark, likely feeling the resistance, released Julie and swam off. It left a fourteen-inch-long bite on her leg and took two-thirds of her calf muscle. The EMS ambulance crew initially took Julie to Roper Hospital in Charleston, but the medical team there transferred her to Emory University Hospital in Atlanta, Georgia. She underwent extensive reconstructive and cosmetic surgery to repair the damage to her leg, and doctors expressed confidence that she would walk again. (Case #GSAF 1985.07.19)

A large tiger shark was confirmed inflicting postmortem bites on the body of fifteen-year-old Kyle Dickens. On August 13, 1995, Kyle was on the beach at Emerald Isle located in Carteret County, North Carolina, when he entered the ocean to rescue a boy who was caught in a riptide. Kyle drowned in his efforts. Two days later, divers recovered his body, which had been inflicted with extreme marine animal damage according to Medical Examiner John L. Almeida, MD (Case #GSAF 1995.08.13)

The International Shark Attack File (ISAF), started by the U.S. Navy in the 1960s and now headquartered at the Florida Museum of Natural History in Gainesville, Florida, has on record a tiger shark incident that occurred in 1996 somewhere in North Carolina involving a surfer. The only information available concerning this account is that the victim survived. (Case #GSAF 1996.00.00a)

One of the most vicious shark attacks in recent history occurred on the east coast of the United States; experts believe that it was the work of a tiger shark. Other investigators claim that a bull shark was involved: On September 3, 2001, twenty-eight-year-old Russian computer programmer Sergei Zaloukaev and his girlfriend, twenty-three-year-old graduate student Natalia Slobodskaya, were vacationing at Avon, a remote town on the Outer Banks of North Carolina, where they had rented a cottage for the Labor Day weekend. With them were friends Josh Granger, Yana Gorbalenya, and another person. Early that evening, the five friends decided to go swimming just off the beach at Greenwood Place in the Askins Creek area of Avon. The water was murky, and high tide would arrive at 7:44 p.m. Three of the friends decided to go ashore, leaving Sergei and Natalia in the water. The couple was in about six to ten feet of water, approximately two feet apart, swimming in a channel on the seaward side of an inshore sandbar. They had been in the water for five to ten minutes, when at around 6:00 p.m., Natalia felt something big and rough—like sandpaper—scrape her back and legs. She was still processing what had happened, trying to figure out what had scraped her, when she felt something tugging at her from below and behind. At first she thought it was one of their friends trying to scare her, but then Sergei began screaming, "It's a shark! Swim!" It pushed between the couple and grabbed Natalia's upper left thigh and buttock, removing a chunk of flesh to the bone approximately twelve to fifteen inches in diameter. It then grabbed and removed Sergei's right buttock in one swift bite. As the couple struggled to reach shore, screaming in terror, the shark relentlessly continued its attack. It came at them from different directions, first from behind Natalia, then from below her, then at Sergei again. It hit Sergei, severing part of his right leg and a finger; then it lunged at Natalia again, removing her left foot at the ankle. More than once, Natalia shoved the shark with her hands, only to have its teeth slash open her wrist and cut off the tip of her left middle finger. The shark continued its attack on the couple until they reached water too shallow for it to continue. It then swam off. Once in the shallows, the couple continued screaming for assistance. Beachgoers had heard their screams but thought the two were playing, and their friends were too far down the beach to hear their cries. Sergei helped Natalia to shore despite his horrific injuries. The couple's friends soon realized that they were in distress and rushed to their aid. Gary Harkin and his friends Paul and Carolyn Richards were sitting on the beach under a tent when they saw people helping the couple to shore. Gary tried using his long-sleeved T-shirt as a tourniquet on Sergei's leg while Carolyn administered cardiopulmonary resuscitation (CPR). When first responders arrived at the scene, approximately six minutes after the attack, Sergei was in full cardiac arrest. The EMS crew initially transported both victims to a small medical facility in Avon that was simply not prepared for the significant injuries that the couple had sustained. Sergei Zaloukaev was pronounced dead upon arrival, and Natalia Slobodskaya was transported by helicopter to Sentara Norfolk General Hospital in Virginia for emergency care. She survived the attack. (Cases #GSAF 2001.09.03a/b)

Positive identification of the shark species involved in this attack is inconclusive. According to surgeon Jeffrey Riblet, the twelve-inch-diameter section removed from Natalia's left buttock suggests that the attacking shark was at least ten-feet, three-inches long. Some experts suggest that because of the animal's extreme aggression and determination, a bull shark was most likely involved. However, according to Jack Musick of the Virginia Institute of Marine Science:

> Examination of photos of Natalia Slobodskaya's injuries show that virtually her entire left buttock was removed by one very clean symmetrical bite suggesting teeth in the upper and lower jaws of the shark were similar. Likewise, the left foot was cleanly bitten off, the tibia popped at the joint suggesting the shark rolled as it bit. Given the size of the bite (at least 12" across) and the symmetrical nature of the bite and the apparent rolling behavior, the most likely species was the tiger shark (*Galeocerdo cuvieri*).[37]

In personal correspondence, ISAF Director George H. Burgess stated, "Based on available evidence, we cannot positively identify the species involved in the 2001 North Carolina attack. However, my best guesstimate is that the attacking species was a tiger shark. All indications are that a single shark was involved."

Aside from the symmetrical bite that suggests similar teeth in the upper and lower jaws, another piece of evidence directly pointing to a tiger shark is the fact that tigers have a history of attacking more than one victim at a time. For example, see the two encounters cited below.

On October 27, 1937, a tiger shark killed Norman Girvan and Jack Brinkley at Kirra Beach, Coolangatta, Australia. Gordon Doniger was next to Norman when the shark first struck. It grabbed Norman by the leg and shook him forcibly. Norman was pulled from Gordon's arms and dragged under. During this time, Gordon saw Jack Brinkley swimming close by and called out to him for help. As Jack was swimming toward them, the shark struck him. Norman Girvan was never found, but portions of his body later washed ashore. Jack Brinkley sustained severe lacerations to his left side, and his left arm was almost completely amputated. He died at the hospital. (Cases #GSAF 1937.10.27a/b)

On November 20, 2017, forty-nine-year-old Rohina Bhandari was diving in Isla Coco National Park, Costa Rica. She was with a group of eighteen people onboard the *MV Sea Hunter*, a 115-foot vessel designed for long-distance diving expeditions, at a site known as Manuelita. While the group was underwater, the twenty-six-year-old male, divemaster Jimenez witnessed a tiger shark approaching them. He attempted to scare it away as the group made for the surface. The shark followed and attacked Rohina at the surface, severely biting her legs. Jimenez attempted to intervene; the shark attacked him, as well. EMS workers removed Rohina from the water; she died en route to Puntarenas, which was thirty-six hours away by boat. Divemaster Jimenez was taken to the hospital and was last reported to be in stable condition and conscious. (Cases #GSAF 2017.11.30a/b)

The following incident involving a tiger shark is one that I categorized as a "shark attack prior to death not ruled out or confirmed (SAPTDU)." A medical examiner originally ruled it as a fatal shark attack but later retracted that ruling, replacing it with drowning as the official cause of death.

On September 12, 2009, Richard Alan Snead, age sixty, and his wife Helen Snead, age fifty-eight, of Pittsburgh, Pennsylvania, were vacationing with family and friends at 501 Conch Crescent located in the Ocean Sands Section B of Corolla, North Carolina. It was their first day of vacation, and at around 7:00 p.m., Richard left the house to go for a walk on the beach. He returned from his walk at approximately 9:00 p.m. and changed into blue and green swim trunks. As he was exiting the house, heading for the beach carrying a red towel, he passed by his wife Helen; his friend, Patricia Phillips; and six other women who at the time were sitting in a hot tub. At around 10:00 p.m., Helen returned to her room to unpack, settle down, and read a book. While she was reading, she started to worry that her husband had not returned from his swim. She began looking for a flashlight to search the beach for him but couldn't find one. She decided to hit the beach anyway; once there, she started calling out her husband's name. Soon, other members of the group who were staying in the home joined her, and they all began walking the beach looking for Richard. Patricia Phillips was not part of that group (she had later stated that her friends had woken her up around midnight, telling her that Richard had not returned and that they were heading for the beach to look for him). Approximately fifteen minutes later, they called 911. At around 12:15 a.m. on September 13, Currituck County Sheriff's Officer J. I. Taylor received a call for a missing person at 501 Conch Crescent. Law enforcement, fire and rescue, ocean rescue, and the U.S. Coast Guard were also contacted for assistance, and all units remained on scene until approximately 5:30 a.m. At that time, officials decided to suspend the search until daylight. At about 7:00 a.m., all aforementioned agencies returned to resume the search. The Currituck County Sheriff's Office estimated that Richard Snead had entered the water near Mile Post 5 sometime around 10:30 p.m. in Corolla on September 12. His glasses and towel were found on the beach. An MH-60 Jayhawk helicopter crew from the U.S. Coast Guard Air Station Elizabeth City and a forty-seven-foot rescue boat crew from Station Oregon were also used to look for Richard. The search continued into late Sunday evening until officials decided to call it off indefinitely.

Five days later, on September 17, 2009, a vacationer out for an early morning walk discovered a man's body washed ashore in the 1300 block of North Virginia Dare Trail in Kill Devil Hills, North Carolina. On the following day, the North Carolina Office of the Chief Medical Examiner in Greenville confirmed that the body's identity was Richard Alan Snead.

Police estimate that Snead's body washed ashore twenty to twenty-five miles south of where he had entered the water. The medical examiner determined that Richard had died of massive blood loss due to a shark bite. According to an autopsy assistant at the Brody School of Medicine at East Carolina University, "Snead suffered extensive injuries, and there is no question that a shark attack caused his death. Living tissue looks different when it receives an injury, versus tissues that are already dead."

During my investigation the first thing I asked the law enforcement officer who was working the recovery scene regarded evidence of any possible slash wounds on the inner hands. He told me that he used to work homicide and that this was the first thing he noticed about the body. He said that, judging from the injuries to the hand, it looked as though the victim had suffered defenselike wounds—similar to ones the officer had seen on victims fending off a knife-wielding attacker. The inner left hand had sustained multiple lacerations, and the corpse was missing the right hand. Missing hands or fingers are often the result of defense wounds in shark attack cases. These were additional indications that the victim indeed had been struggling with something prior to death.

After examining on-scene and autopsy photos, the investigation report, and the medical examiner's report, shark experts with the Global Shark Attack File made the following statement:

It appeared a shark may have initially grasped the victim's lower extremities, or possibly his torso or right leg, while he was still alive. The wounds visible on the lower extremities may have been survivable if the victim could have been rescued and had then received immediate proper medical attention, but also likely, these wounds could have led to panic and drowning. The slanted tooth marks in the leg point to a tiger shark as the attacking species. The shark's probable removal of the missing oil-rich organs from the torso also suggests a tiger shark's involvement; however, other marine organisms scavenged on the body as well. A tiger shark frequently grabs prey on the surface, then submerges, and, using its wide snout, pushes its prey item into the sand or a crevice as it feeds. The intact face/head of the deceased and its discoloration suggests this may have been the case with the deceased's body; his body spent time on the seafloor immediately after death. The victim seems to have attempted to defend himself, possibly trying to push the shark away or pry open the shark's jaws thus resulting in the defense wounds on the right hand and the missing left hand. The shark most likely submerged and pulled the victim below the surface where he [the victim] would have quickly lost consciousness. There was considerable dolphin activity on the day the deceased disappeared and on the following day, which suggests schools of fish were present, and at such times there are invariably large numbers of sharks in the area as well. The deceased entered the water after dusk, a time when many species of sharks feed closer to shore. Due to the paucity of remains, a forensic analysis of the sequence of events prior to finding the body is not possible. However, due to what little evidence can be gleaned from the remains, together with the circumstances surrounding the deceased's disappearance, the medical examiner's initial opinion appears the most likely scenario, that the deceased was attacked by a shark, which resulted in drowning and death. (GSAF)

Not long after the official cause of death was released, a couple of other shark researchers not affiliated with the Global Shark Attack File examined photos of the body. They attributed cause of death to either drowning or a heart-related issue and concluded that the shark bites on the body were postmortem. After that evaluation, the medical examiner decided to change the cause of death to drowning. Later the same day, after a telephone conversation with me, the medical examiner's office reverted its decision to the original shark attack scenario as the cause of death, pending further investigation. Eventually, the medical examiner made the final decision to change the official cause of death from shark attack to accidental drowning. (Case #GSAF 2009.09.12)

Some researchers and officials will label the cause of death as a shark attack only if there are witnesses to the accident or if there is a survivor. These same officials are also very quick to state the cause of death as drowning in cases similar to this one, when the cause is actually undetermined because scientific evidence is also pointing to another potential or plausible cause of death, such as shark attack. Occasionally, investigators must be wary of conclusions from professionals who may be influenced by political, financial, or other factors regarding a shark attack account. I once experienced an attempt to conceal shark bite evidence. On another occasion, interviewees led me astray during an investigation into a historical account. Input from experts and officials is always welcomed as a necessary part of an inquiry into any shark-related incident; however, the obligation to follow the facts—wherever they may lead—must remain the highest priority, not only as a service to the victim and their family but also for the preservation of historical accuracy as the case is entered into the global database.

A shark attack harms coastal community businesses, and it can cast a dark shadow on sharks in general, so it is understandable why shark advocates as well as business owners and local politicians wouldn't want a shark to take the rap for a death or injury that could be in question. Equally important, there is no need for someone to shout "shark attack" for every situation that mirrors this case. Investigators must honestly and thoroughly evaluate the scientific evidence presented in these incidents in a fair, unbiased manner in order to present a best possible scenario regarding each cause of death. In my opinion, the evidence in this case points to a shark attack prior to death. The medical examiner initially concurred with this, and GSAF scientists maintain this opinion.

Shark attack survivor Al Brenneka shared his perspective when he commented on a shark attack survivors' board regarding this case. According to Al:

> I arrived at the hospital DOA, and if I had not been revived,
> my cause of death would have been ruled the same as Richard
> Snead. I was ripped off my surfboard and taken underwater by
> the shark. I fought with the shark in turmoil of water at the sur-
> face, and these things caused my lungs to have enough water in

them for me to have been considered drowned. I had two tubes inserted into my lungs and had several weeks of treatment to remove all the water from my lungs. If a shark attack caused my lungs to have water in them and I had a surfboard for flotation, it is very possible for sharks to have the ability to drown people in other incidents before death or cause a drowning death. [. . . If] I wasn't able to get the shark to let go and died as the shark was removing flesh from my arm, the tissue proving I was alive at the time of the attack would have been removed and leaving tissue that would have proved I would have been scavenged by a shark. The difference between a shark attack fatality and a drowning can be a few seconds. The difference between a shark attack fatality and a scavenged body can be one bite away.[38]

The following fatal report involving a tiger shark is another case where the cause of death is in question; therefore, I have listed this incident as another "shark attack prior to death not ruled out or confirmed (SAPTDU)." I collected details on this incident through personally corresponding with Professor Frank J. Schwartz and conversing with a search-and-rescue diver from New Hanover County, North Carolina. The *Wilmington Morning Star* newspaper (now *StarNews Online)* documented the sequence of events.

....

Doug Nunnally was a forty-nine-year-old teacher at New Hanover High School in Wilmington, North Carolina, when he decided to go out on his boat to dive or spearfish alone on Sunday, October 8, 1989. Earlier that morning, Doug was studying in a Wrightsville Beach house that he and his wife of one-and-a-half years, Maryann, were renting. Maryann said that the last time she talked to her husband was sometime before noon on that Sunday. He had told her that he would return to their Pender County, North Carolina, home by 3:00 p.m. When Doug hadn't arrived home by 3:00 p.m., Maryann wasn't immediately worried because her husband had never been on time for anything in his whole life. Maryann started becoming edgy when Doug hadn't shown up by 3:30 p.m., so she drove to Wrightsville Beach to look for him. She went to the rented house and saw that the lights were on, the radio was playing, and a book was on the desk. He had obviously been there. Next, she went to the slip in Banks Channel, located between two bridges where Doug kept his twenty-foot motorboat. The boat was gone, and after talking with several of his friends at the beach, Maryann learned that he had left in the boat sometime between 2:30 p.m. and 4:00 p.m. At around 5:00 p.m., she called the U.S. Coast Guard. Officers with the Coast Guard later placed his departure sometime between 3:00 p.m. and 3:15 p.m., although Maryann and the officers said that no one could clarify exactly when he had left. When last spotted by neighbors, Doug was headed south along the channel and had apparently told one of them that he was going to get some fish. Doug was a certified diver, so Maryann thought that her husband may have been going to spearfish under the Causeway Bridge as he had done in the past. However, a good friend who had dived often with him said he doubted that Doug was going spearfishing. There was a northeast wind blowing hard that day, and water visibility had been bad since Hurricane Hugo. Doug was last seen wearing a black wetsuit. He was an excellent diver and, according to friends, had never experienced any problems with the sport. Doug's friend Wayne Holden took to the water searching for him most of Sunday night and Monday. Coast Guard crews searched by helicopter and by ship, and a U.S. Marine Corps helicopter also joined the search. By Monday afternoon, two Coast Guard ships were searching the ocean, and one was searching the waterway and marshes. A third helicopter also joined the search. As of 11:30 p.m. on October 9, 1989, no one had found Doug's boat or any sign of Doug.[39]

On Tuesday, October 10, 1989, the Coast Guard received a report from a pleasure boater saying that they saw a boat drifting near Frying Pan Shoals. The Coast Guard found the boat drifting about four miles southeast of the shoals at 6:27 p.m. Authorities identified the drifting boat—a 1963 Thunderbird named *Jo-Ann*—as belonging to Doug Nunnally, and his wallet was found aboard. Officials also found a pair of pants and a tank of compressed air used for diving. The keys were in the ignition, and the boat was in neutral. The boat was not damaged, there were no signs of an injury or a struggle by Doug, and there was no evidence of anyone else having been on board. The anchor was out, and the line was longer than the depth of the water in which the boat was found, indicating that Doug had tried to anchor somewhere deeper. Doug's friends told Coast Guard officials that it was a common practice for Doug and other divers to anchor off shipwrecks by diving down to attach the anchor to the wreck. However, there were no wrecks in the immediate area where the boat was found. Coast Guard personnel think that the boat may have drifted for a while prior to being found. The Coast Guard searched throughout the night using a helicopter equipped with an infrared heat-seeking device that picks up body heat and is used by search and rescue teams to locate people lost at sea. Everyone hoped that because Doug may have been wearing a wetsuit, he may still have been alive, floating somewhere in the ocean.[40]

The search for Doug continued through October 11 and 12, 1989, by Coast Guard helicopters and ships. His diver friends also continued searching, diving in areas that Doug often visited, but they found no indication that he had been there. Since the beginning of the search, ships and helicopters had covered 5,750 square miles of ocean from Morehead City, North Carolina, to Georgetown, South Carolina. Teams also continually searched the Atlantic Intracoastal Waterway from Swansboro, North Carolina, to Little River, South Carolina, and up the Cape Fear River into North Carolina. On October 13, 1989, at about 1:10 p.m., officials suspended the search for Doug Nunnally. Friends and family were upset and bewildered by his disappearance, especially considering his twenty years of diving experience. No one could understand why Doug would go diving by himself.[41]

On Sunday, October 15, 1989, two fishermen spotted a body about six miles east of Carolina Beach Inlet. They tied a line to it until the Coast Guard arrived. A search-and-rescue diver for New Hanover County, North Carolina, told me years later that he had been working on the day the body had been found. This diver was not deployed to the recovery scene, but his partners were. They recovered only a portion of spinal cord and a lower torso. The divers onsite attributed the cause of death to a shark bite. The portion of the recovered corpse was also still wearing part of a black wetsuit similar to the one that Doug was last seen wearing.[42] The medical examiner was able to positively identify the body as being Doug Nunnally from surgical scars on his spine. The medical examiner could not determine how long Doug had been in the water before dying or what caused his death; however, it appeared that a shark had attacked the forty-nine-year-old at some point. After finding no suspicious circumstances about Doug's death, the New Hanover County Sheriff's Department closed his case. Coast Guard officials speculated that Doug's disappearance may have started when he dove into the water to tie his anchor to a shipwreck.[43] Photos of Doug Nunnally's body were sent to Professor Frank J. Schwartz of the Institute of Marine Sciences at UNC Chapel Hill. After examining the photos, Schwartz attributed this incident to a tiger shark.[44] Doug Nunnally's death certificate officially states that his date of death was October 8, 1989. The document cites the immediate cause of death as "undetermined" and the manner of death as an "accident."[45] (Case #GSAF 1989.10.08)

Bull Shark
(*Carcharhinus leucas*)

The species that make up "the deadly trio" of the shark world have attacked and killed more people than have any other shark species. The white shark leads the three with the most recorded attacks, and the tiger shark follows in second. The bull shark takes third place; however, most researchers today believe that the bull shark is the most dangerous shark—and for good reason: Bull sharks are likely responsible for many attacks blamed on the great white and tiger sharks, and the bull shark could be the species behind numerous incidents where the attacking species is officially listed as "unidentified."

The *bull shark* is a stout, thick-bodied animal, dull gray in color, with small, beady eyes that are set forward on a wide, rounded snout.

It likes to prowl along the bottom of the seafloor, seldom approaching the surface, as it hunts the ocean's shallow surf zone, stalking its prey within inlets, estuaries, and even far up rivers. Because of its preference for the ocean shallows and its tendency to penetrate inland waters, it is more likely to encounter people than the white shark or tiger shark. The bull shark also likes to hunt in murky water, where sight doesn't play as pivotal a role in its hunting strategy as do sensing movements and vibrations and following its sense of smell. A bull shark will also engage in physical contact prior to attacking, using a bump-and-bite tactic and striking its snout against a targeted interest to determine whether it wants to take a bite. The upper teeth are broad and triangular, with course, serrated edges, whereas the lower teeth are narrower and more finely serrated. Together, these two sets of teeth are more than capable of removing large amounts of flesh from target prey in a single bite. The bull shark is an extremely aggressive species and may easily become agitated if other animals or people compromise its space. It regularly hunts other sharks, dolphins, turtles, a variety of fish, or anything that crosses its path. A bull shark will not hesitate to take on large prey—even larger than themselves. One bull shark was reported to have attacked a horse in the Brisbane River of South East Queensland, Australia, and another took on a group of hippos in South Africa's iSimangaliso Wetland Park.[46] Although not scientifically proven to have the highest testosterone levels of any animal, as some reports have suggested, bull sharks are still prone to truculence and have made numerous verified attacks on bathers, surfers, divers, and fishermen—with several such incidents proving fatal. I have investigated a number of bull shark attacks in the Carolinas and one in Texas. Bull sharks are serious predators that deserve much respect, and swimmers should be educated on how to decrease their chances of an encounter with one.

Bull sharks average in size from six to eleven feet in length and can tip the scales at more than five hundred pounds. In 2009, researchers captured a massive pregnant female bull shark more than three miles inland from the sea up the Breede River in South Africa. That shark was thirteen feet long and weighed 1,000 pounds. Large specimens have also been caught in the Carolinas—including a three-hundred-pounder taken from Johnnie Mercers Fishing Pier

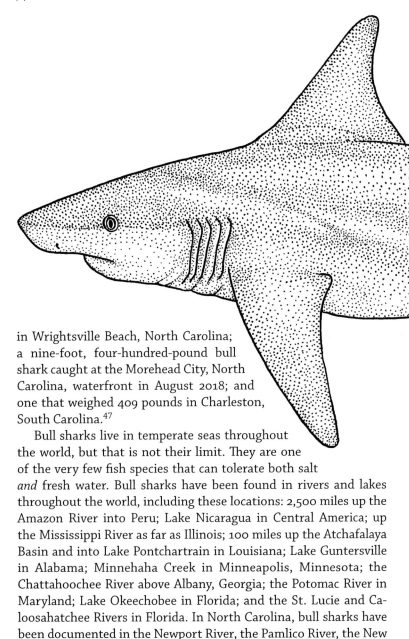

in Wrightsville Beach, North Carolina;
a nine-foot, four-hundred-pound bull
shark caught at the Morehead City, North
Carolina, waterfront in August 2018; and
one that weighed 409 pounds in Charleston,
South Carolina.[47]

Bull sharks live in temperate seas throughout
the world, but that is not their limit. They are one
of the very few fish species that can tolerate both salt
and fresh water. Bull sharks have been found in rivers and lakes
throughout the world, including these locations: 2,500 miles up the
Amazon River into Peru; Lake Nicaragua in Central America; up
the Mississippi River as far as Illinois; 100 miles up the Atchafalaya
Basin and into Lake Pontchartrain in Louisiana; Lake Guntersville
in Alabama; Minnehaha Creek in Minneapolis, Minnesota; the
Chattahoochee River above Albany, Georgia; the Potomac River in
Maryland; Lake Okeechobee in Florida; and the St. Lucie and Ca-
loosahatchee Rivers in Florida. In North Carolina, bull sharks have
been documented in the Newport River, the Pamlico River, the New

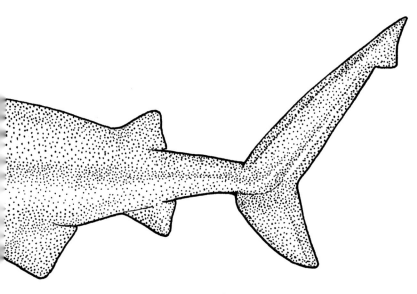

River near Jacksonville, the Neuse River above New Bern, the Cape Fear River near Wilmington, and the Northeast Cape Fear River above Wilmington. In the 1980s, two large bull sharks were caught just downriver from Union Point Park in New Bern, and in 2011, researchers tagged an eight-footer in the Neuse River.[48] River workers have spotted them in the Pamlico River near Belhaven and as far up the Pamlico River as Chocowinity.[49] I talked to a fisherman who claims to have caught two bull sharks on bush hooks that he had set for catfish in the Northeast Cape Fear River just up from the Whitestocking Road state boating access in Pender County one August. Another avid catfisherman who works as a North Carolina State Highway Patrol officer told me that he fishes the Northeast Cape Fear River and has heard of sharks being caught there—south of the Highway 210 Bridge in Castle Hayne, New Hanover County—during the summer months.

Bull sharks are abundant in both Carolinas, inshore and offshore, with records of their capture from January through December. They appear most commonly in the warmer months of May through

October and may pup their young in Carolina waters in May or June. This amazing shark species could potentially be inhabiting any body of water throughout the Carolinas.

Attacks by bull sharks in the Carolinas have been verified, and several more incidents (discussed below) were likely caused by bull sharks but still cannot be positively identified as such. Other attacks in both North and South Carolina that officials blamed on other species may also have been caused by bull sharks. In the following shark bite cases, bull sharks were either verified or were likely to have been involved.

On Saturday, September 21, 1935, Jere W. Fountain, Jim Collins, and Jim's father-in-law, Paul Ventors, made plans to camp from Saturday night through Sunday on an island located in Brown's Inlet on the New River at Onslow Beach, which is about ten miles from Jacksonville, North Carolina. Today Marine Corps Base Camp Lejeune occupies that part of the beach. The men were planning to stay in the only house on the beach for a weekend of fishing, swimming, and relaxing. Ned Henderson, a friend of Jere's, owned the house. It was a rustic dwelling with no inside plumbing, electricity, or telephone. The only way for the men to reach the island's beach was for them to cross the inland waterway in a rowboat, so they left Jere's car parked and proceeded to paddle to the campsite. They arrived at the house just before dark that Saturday afternoon. At about 8:30 p.m., the men decided that, before they settled in, they would go for a swim in the waters of Brown's Inlet. They left their clothes on the beach and entered the water. Jere was wading about ten feet from the others in waist-deep water when suddenly Jim and Paul heard Jere call out, "Help me; something struck me!" They rushed to Jere immediately, and he fainted in their arms. They carried him to shore and laid him on the sand, discovering that something had bitten a huge section out of his thigh, nearly severing his leg above the knee. They quickly tore Jere's clothes into strips and made a tourniquet for his leg—to stop the bleeding. Jim then left his father-in-law with Jere, took the rowboat across the waterway, got into Jere's car, and went to get help. Jim, in his haste and excitement, ran the car into a tree and wrecked it. He then thumbed a ride from a man in a pickup truck. Jim asked the man to let him drive and told him that he had to get to a doctor in Jacksonville quickly. Several hours had passed before Jim Collins and Dr. John Henderson (a medical doctor from Jacksonville) could return to the shark attack site. Upon arrival, they learned that Jere had died minutes after Jim had left—about ten minutes after the shark bite had occurred. Dr. Henderson and Jere's friends spent hours transporting Jere's body across the waterway in the boat and to the funeral home in Jacksonville.

At 4:00 a.m. on Sunday, Jim, Dr. Henderson, and Jere's sister-in-law Hazel Mizelle arrived at Jere's home to deliver the terrible news to his family. The doctor said that the shark had severed the main artery in Jere's leg and that Jere had bled to death. Dr. Henderson theorized that a shark had come near shore possibly because fishermen had thrown food into the water at that location. Coroner Kimmon Jones stated that the toothprints of a shark were plainly visible on Jere's body but that sharks didn't typically frequent the inlet. Investigators did not identify the shark species involved in this incident; however, considering the location of the attack, the depth of water where it occurred, and the victim's significant injury, a bull shark was likely the attacking species.[50] (Case #GSAF 1935.09.21)

....

The following details concerning this next case were kindly given to me by David Batterson, a U.S. Navy corpsman stationed on Ocracoke from 1943 to 1945. He was there on the day of the incident.

....

According to David, the attack took place on or one day after May 8, 1945, Victory in Europe (V-E) Day, when Germany officially surrendered at the end of World War II in Europe. Most of the personnel at the amphibious training base had been given the day off to go to the beach. Trucks were transporting people to the one "nice beach" to which they had access. A young Navy seaman stationed at Ocracoke named John Kuntsler was one of the men enjoying the ocean that day. He entered the water along the beach near where the Ocracoke Island airport stands today. It was late in the afternoon, and John headed out past the breakers about fifty or more yards off the beach. In an instant, witnesses heard him yelling, screaming, and calling for help. They watched a trail of blood form on the water, and by the time the rescuers could reach him and take him to shore, he had lost a great deal of blood from a huge gash to his thigh area. C. Felix Harvey was one of the naval officers who witnessed the attack. He remembers helping John get out of the water but said he was dead before the ambulance could get him to the infirmary. David Batterson was late in arriving to the beach, and as he was approaching the oceanfront, another truck passed him, racing back toward the naval base. John was being rushed to the base dispensary for immediate medical aid. By the time John arrived at the dispensary, he had lost so much blood that the doctor couldn't find a vein through which he could administer plasma. At the time, people speculated as to whether the animal that killed John was a barracuda or a shark. David saw official U.S. Navy photos of the victim at the time of his death, and he claimed that a shark killed John because of the wound's size. Witness C. Felix Harvey said that the shark bit John twice. The first bite was to the lower leg, and it went to the bone. The second bite was to the thigh muscle. At 13 inches wide, it nearly severed the leg.

According to David, the Navy intelligence officer at the time of the incident was Aycock Brown, who possibly might have further information on the attack if his records are still available. David told me that he did not know the victim personally, but others had told him that John had been on ships during the landing of troops in the invasion of Europe that, on two occasions, had been sunk by enemy fire. "How ironic to have survived those incidents and to die so close to the end of the war," David said. Naval Officer C. Felix Harvey had compiled a report of this attack and any other similar cases that may have occurred in the area. Unfortunately that report has been lost.

Officials did not verify the attacking species in this Ocracoke case, and rumors circulated that a white shark was the culprit. However, because of proximity to shore, time of year, and wound severity, a bull shark is the most likely suspect. (Case #GSAF 1945.05.08)

On August 15, 1993, a bull shark about seven feet long was involved in the attack on nineteen-year-old Petra Rijoes, a student at North Carolina State University. The teenager was seriously injured around 10:00 a.m. She was riding a flotation device that was being pulled by her father's thirty-five-foot sailboat near Brant Island Shoal in the brackish backwaters of the Pamlico Sound, about midway between Bay River and Ocracoke Inlet, North Carolina. Petra was holding onto a rope, enjoying being towed on her float, when she was suddenly hit from below. The shark, likely cruising the bottom, spotted the movement at the surface, which triggered a predatory response. Professor Frank J. Schwartz, a well-respected shark expert with the UNC Institute of Marine Sciences in Morehead City, North Carolina, speculated that the shark may have been trying to get out of the inlet into cooler water and could have been agitated by the warmer waters and also by the wake of the boat. Petra sustained severe injuries across her lower abdomen, near her genitals, and across one leg. The injuries required more than 300 stitches. EMS transported her to Carteret General Hospital (now Carteret Health Care Medical Center), where she received treatment and recovered from her injuries before returning to school.[51] (Case #GSAF 1993.08.15a)

On the same weekend, there was an unconfirmed report of a shark swimming in North Carolina's Currituck Sound near the Wright Memorial Bridge. Eleven days after the incident, a commercial fisherman found a seven-and-a-half-foot, 260-pound bull shark in his flounder nets four hundred feet south of the Wright Memorial Bridge. Over the years, prior to this incident, commercial fishermen had caught at least three bull sharks, each approximately six feet long, in the Croatan Sound in Dare County, North Carolina. For shark investigators, analyzing contiguous details regarding both the historical and any current patterns exhibited by each species can be significant when determining shark involvement in an incident.

On July 20, 2002, at around 5:00 p.m., fifteen-year-old Mary Katherine Strong and her parents had arrived for vacation on the 660 block of Ocean Drive at Emerald Isle, North Carolina. While her parents were unpacking their car, Mary Katherine headed to the water for a quick swim. She was in the water for about five minutes when she felt something bite her leg. She exited the water on her own and was taken to the emergency room (ER) at Carteret General Hospital (now Carteret Health Care Medical Center). Later, Mary Katherine was transferred to Duke University Medical Center in Durham for surgery to repair damage to her calf. She sustained considerable tissue damage, but no bones were broken or fractured. Professor Frank J. Schwartz of the UNC Institute of Marine Sciences analyzed photographs of Mary Katherine's leg wound and confirmed that a bull shark measuring around six to seven feet long and weighing in at approximately 190 pounds was responsible for the attack. (Case #GSAF 2002.07.20)

On Labor Day, September 5, 2005, eighteen-year-old Elizabeth Gardner, her boyfriend Forrest Powell, and family had gone to North Topsail Beach, Onslow County, North Carolina, for a day's vacation. Elizabeth and Forrest entered the water at the mouth of New River Inlet near Onslow Beach Access No. 3 to wade and play in the waves. They began swimming near a shoal to which people often wade at low tide, located five hundred to six hundred yards from shore. The water was a murky brownish-blue in color, and the very uneven seafloor could change from ankle-deep to waist-deep water quickly. Elizabeth and Forrest had been in the water approximately fifteen to twenty minutes and were about three hundred feet from shore when, at 2:30 p.m., Elizabeth turned toward shore to hug her boyfriend. At that point, she felt something grab her right leg. She felt three bites that lasted all of three seconds. She lifted her right leg out of the water, and when she saw her wound, she started screaming. Forrest picked her up and carried her almost the entire way to shore. When he got her close to the beach, three men met him in the water and carried Elizabeth the rest of the way. On the beach, about ten people gathered around Elizabeth, some of them putting towels under her leg. Someone placed a tourniquet on her leg, but an EMS worker who happened to be on the beach at the time told them to take it off. She was in and out of consciousness during this time. An ambulance soon arrived, and Elizabeth was taken to Naval Medical Center Camp Lejeune, where she was given morphine. Hospital staff attempted to clean the wound, but she was in too much pain for them to continue. She stayed at the hospital for about three-and-a-half hours, and then an ambulance crew transported her to Pitt County Memorial Hospital in Greenville, North Carolina, for emergency surgery.

The bite was severe. Elizabeth sustained tendon, muscle, tissue, and skin loss to the lower posterior right leg. The Achilles tendon was damaged. The wounds extended from the right heel to halfway up her calf. There was a quarter-sized hole just above her right ankle and tooth impressions along the posterior right foot. To close the wounds, surgeons administered twenty-one centimeters of sutures, but they left the hole above the ankle open to drain. From wound photos that Elizabeth provided to me, shark experts deduced that a six-foot bull shark was most likely responsible for the attack. (Case #GSAF 2005.09.05)

On June 26, 2011, ten-year-old Cassidy Cartwright and her mother were boogie boarding in the water at North Topsail Beach, Onslow County, North Carolina. Hundreds of people were on the beach, and more than fifty people were swimming in the water near them. The water was murky, and underwater visibility was minimal. Cassidy and her mother had been standing in the same spot for about fifteen minutes—facing seaward in about three-and-a-half feet of water—when Cassidy suddenly felt something tugging on her leg. She did not immediately feel any pain, but the animal pulled her down into the water. At first, she thought someone was playing around, but then the animal pulled her down once again. She was not submerged under the water, but she felt the shark bite her once, let go, and then bite her a second time. Cassidy's mother saw her stumble and went to help her up. She then noticed blood pooling in the water from her daughter's injury and quickly pulled Cassidy to shore with help from a friend. Something had bitten Cassidy on her right ankle. The bite severed her Achilles tendon and two muscles—the *peroneus brevis* and the *peroneus*—which together function in allowing outward rotation of the sole of the foot. Cassidy's mother wrapped the injury with beach towels to slow the blood loss. Emergency personnel arrived and transported her to an ambulance. The EMS crew took her to a field, where an airlift team picked her up. The airlift team flew her to New Hanover Regional Medical Center in Wilmington, North Carolina. Later, another ambulance transported her to UNC Chapel Hill for surgery.

Surgeons recovered a tooth fragment from Cassidy's injury. I sent photos of the fragment—along with a case report—to the Shark Research Institute for study. Dr. Gordon Hubbell, an expert in shark dentition, evaluated the photos, and relayed the following comments to me. I added these comments to the final case report.

I have studied the pictures of the tooth fragment, and the following are my comments:

1. I have examined the pattern of the serrations and the number of serrations and they are consistent with *Carcharhinus leucas* [bull shark]. They are definitely not *Carcharodon carcharias* or *Carcharhinus plumbeus*.

2. Regarding the total length of the shark, upon comparing the size of the tooth fragment with teeth from Bull Sharks of known size, I would estimate that the shark was around 6 feet long (total length).

3. I am surprised that the tooth crown was broken like it was. It tells me that the shark bit with a lot of force. It was not

just a test bite to determine the identity of the object in the water.

Conclusion: This young lady was bitten by a Bull Shark, *Carcharhinus leucas,* approximately 6 feet (180 cm) in total length. (Case #GSAF 2011.06.26)

On July 19, 2011, six-year-old Lucy Mangum was playing in the water on a two-and-a-half-foot boogie board with her sister and with her mother, Jordan. The three of them were at Ocracoke, North Carolina, near Ramp 72 in the South Point area. The sea on that Tuesday was calm and a clear bluish-green in color. They had spent about twenty to thirty minutes in the water and were approximately six feet from shore. At about 5:15 p.m., Lucy was lying prone on her boogie board in about eighteen inches of water facing shoreward, when a shark approached from behind and bit her on the right leg twice. Witnesses reported seeing the shark attacking the girl. Jordan was about ten feet from her daughter when she heard her scream. Jordan turned toward Lucy just in time to see the shark appear right next to her daughter. She reached Lucy and immediately removed her from the water. Using both her hands, Jordan applied pressure to Lucy's wounds. Lucy's father, Craig Mangum—who is an ER doctor—later described Lucy's wound to investigators: "The entire lower leg, mid-calf down, was basically filleted." Craig knew the injuries to his daughter were significant and required treatment at a Level I trauma center. An ambulance crew transported Lucy to a helicopter, and that crew flew her to Pitt County Memorial Hospital in Greenville, North Carolina. She arrived one hour after the attack and underwent surgery. Lucy sustained severe lacerations to her calf, ankle, and foot. She sustained injuries to one of the major vessels supplying blood to the foot and leg. She also had a 90 percent muscle and tendon tear and a severed artery. Lucy was fortunate in that the shark removed no tissue.

Local experts believed that this incident involved a juvenile tiger shark; however, shark dentition expert Dr. Gordon

Hubbell with the Shark Research Institute reported that he and his team strongly suspected that a five-and-a-half-foot bull shark was the attacking species—based on bull sharks' tendency to inhabit shallow water, to be aggressive, and to make lesions similar to those seen on the girl's calf. (Case #GSAF 2011.07.19)

On August 11, 2013, ten-year-old Tyson Royston was shaken but unharmed when his surfboard leash string got tangled up with an eight-foot-long bull shark. Tyson was participating in the two-day South Carolina Governor's Cup of Surfing competition, held at the northern end of Folly Beach, South Carolina, with 225 other surfers. At around 5:15 p.m., Tyson was in the water doing tricks with his board when the shark suddenly appeared and became entangled in the leash. Tyson's coach was standing nearby and saw him struggling. The shark threw Tyson into a wave and pulled him backward and under. Tyson quickly unhooked his leash and swam for shore in haste. Two other surfers and five lifeguards helped get him safely to shore. People had reported numerous shark sightings that day, and after Tyson's very close call, the remainder of the competition was rescheduled for September.[52] (Case #GSAF 2013.08.11)

Two of the worst North Carolina attacks of 2015 happened on June 14, in the waters off the tranquil coastal community of Oak Island, and as you will see, the bull shark species remains the culprit.

At approximately 4:40 p.m. on June 14, 2015, twelve-year-old Kiersten Yow from Archdale was swimming with her cousin and several people in waist-deep water in front of the Ocean Crest Motel next to the Ocean Crest Fishing Pier when she was severely bitten by a shark. She said she remembers feeling something bump her prior to being bitten, and during the attack she remembers punching the shark three times before getting pulled from the water. Her left arm below the elbow was amputated, and she suffered a large bite near the back upper thigh of her left leg exposing the bone. A large portion of flesh was removed from her leg, but the femoral artery was not damaged. Paramedic Marie Hildreth from Charlotte was fortunately nearby and rushed to help the girl. She used strings from a boogie board and a tent to help stop blood loss. Bystanders on the beach and first responders helped save Kiersten's life. Her injuries were life-threatening and without their assistance could have proved fatal. She was airlifted to New Hanover Regional Medical Center before being transferred to a hospital in Chapel Hill. (Case #GSAF 2015.06.14a)

On the same day, about two miles down the strand, an incident occurred in the Oak Island area of North Carolina, near the beach access at SE 55th Street, which is about halfway between Ocean Crest Fishing Pier and Oak Island Pier. Three family members from Colorado Springs were enjoying the beach, playing in the surf, and building sandcastles: sixteen-year-old Hunter Treschel, his grandmother Kathryn Lyons, and his cousin Jacob Sward. It was getting late and the tide was beginning to come in, so the three decided to pack up and head back to their motel for the evening. Covered in sand, Hunter and Jacob got back into the ocean one last time to rinse off before leaving. At approximately 5:50 p.m., the boys were wading in waist-deep water. They were in the ocean for only a minute when Hunter felt something beneath the surface bump his left calf. He thought it felt as though a big fish had run into him, so he quickly moved away from it. Again, he felt something bump into him, and then suddenly he was grabbed by the left arm. To his amazement, Hunter saw a shark latched onto his arm halfway up to his bicep. In an instant, the shark was gone—and so was most of Hunter's left arm below the shoulder, along with two-thirds of his bicep. In her account to investigators, Kathryn explained that she had been gathering their things and preparing to leave when she heard someone yelling. She looked seaward toward her grandchildren, who were quickly exiting the water, Jacob's left arm across Hunter's back. She noticed the bewildered look in Hunter's eyes, and the blood-mixed water trailing behind them. When they reached the shore, fellow beachgoers came to Hunter's aid; they did everything they could to help stop the bleeding. When first responders arrived on scene, they moved Hunter out of the path of a passing storm and continued working to stop the bleeding. Hunter's injury was life-threatening, and without quick actions by beachgoers and rescue officials, he could have died. He was airlifted to New Hanover Regional Medical Center in Wilmington and arrived there in serious condition. Medics and hospital personnel transported Hunter to the operating room immediately upon arrival for emergency surgery. He has since recovered and is doing well.[53] (Case #GSAF 2015.06.14b)

....

I arrived at Oak Island, North Carolina, the next morning—on June 15, 2015—to attend a media conference scheduled at 9:00 a.m. Upon arriving I met with local officials—Oak Island Mayor Bettie W. Wallace, Town Manager Tim Holloman, Sheriff John Ingram, and Caswell Beach Mayor Deborah G. Aklers—to discuss the incidents and to offer my assistance on behalf of the Shark Research Institute. According to Sheriff Ingram, beaches were closed after the second attack, and patrol boats and a helicopter were dispatched to the scene. They wanted to determine if any sharks could still be in the area. Around thirty to forty-five minutes after the second attack, the helicopter patrol spotted a shark approximately seven feet long in the area between the two attack sites. A second sighting of a shark was reported further south, and officials confirmed a third sighting just before dark as the animal was heading back out to sea. Sheriff Ingram believes it was the same shark in all three sightings.

I asked the officials about shark-fishing activity on Oak Island because I had heard unconfirmed reports of people chumming from kayaks near the Ocean Crest Fishing Pier on June 12—two days before the attacks had occurred. Island officials confirmed that shark fishing from the beach does occur and likely in conjunction with chumming activity. I told them that I knew of an irresponsible chumming practice that some shark fishermen have been known to use to attract sharks. The reckless activity involves anchoring weighted bags full of fish parts and blood-soaked entrails from kayaks. These bags continue seeping blood into the water for hours off beaches near chosen fishing areas. I stated that if fishermen were engaging in this type of negligent practice on Oak Island, then local officials should intervene and stop it. Irresponsible chumming of that magnitude—if fishermen had indeed been doing it in that area—could have been a contributing factor in attracting large predators at the time of the attacks.

Inquiring about fish activity in the area, I also received confirmation from Oak Island officials and Oak Island Pier employees that schools of bluefish had, in fact, been running all along the beach on the day of the two attacks. Witnesses reported small baitfish in the water at the time of the attacks as well as birds diving that day, both of which indicate fish activity. I also witnessed birds diving at Hunter Treschel's attack site on the following day and saw tiny minnows at the water's edge. Oak Island Pier workers told me that on the day of the two attacks, two jet skiers in the area of Oak Island Pier—which is 4.3 miles north of Ocean Crest Fishing Pier—reported that sharks were everywhere in the water and that pogies were also prevalent in the water along with the bluefish.

On the day before the attacks, I was at Cherry Grove Fishing Pier, located about forty-two miles south of Oak Island. The water was very uninviting that day—murky and thick brown in color. Schools of baitfish populated the breakers up to the shoreline all along the beach. On the day of the attacks, reports indicated that the water was murky and greenish in color, and it was about the same condition at both sites during my investigations the day after.

I submitted a summary of my investigations to Oak Island officials. The report included the following details and recommendations:

Potential Causative Factors Which May Have Contributed to the 2015 Shark Bite Incidents

1. *Swimming in the late afternoon/early evening.* Both victims were swimming in the late afternoon. Studies have shown that swimming at this particular time can increase your chances of encountering a shark because some shark species come closer to shore in search of food the closer it gets to night.
2. *Swimming in murky water.* The water is usually murky off of Oak Island. The day after the attacks, the water was murky

with a greenish color to it. Some species of sharks hunt in murky water, some sharks may bite in murky water due to stress or agitation, and some sharks may be prone to bite in murky water because they may not recognize the object in front of them and bite to find out what it is.

3. *Swimming when schools of fish are in the area.* It has been confirmed that schools of bluefish and pogies were running in the area the day of the attacks. Witnesses also claim they saw birds diving in the area of the second attack. I observed pelicans diving fairly close to shore at the second attack site the day after the attacks on June 15. Diving birds indicate that there are schools of fish in the area, thus increasing the chance of sharks being present as well.

4. *Swimming near a fishing pier.* The first victim was bitten while swimming near a fishing pier. Fishing piers due to structure, constant bait in the water, struggling fish throughout the day and night, and cleaning tables which let fish entrails back into the ocean are areas that are attractive to sharks.

5. *Shark fishing from the beach and possible irresponsible chumming for sharks in the area.* Some news sources mentioned shark fishing from the beach, and I have been told that chumming activity to attract sharks is likely practiced on the island. There was mention of a kayaker dropping chum near the Ocean Crest Pier on Friday before the attacks. Irresponsible fishing practices such as chumming off a public beach can bring predators to the area.

Recommendations to Oak Island and Caswell Beach Officials

1. Drafting a County Ordinance making it unlawful for any person to bait or chum for sharks or any other form of marine life in the area within one mile of a public beach.

2. Patrol officers should monitor the beaches and get an idea of beach shark fishing activity, noting when, where, and at what times this is taking place. If irresponsible chumming activity is observed or suspected, it should be stopped. Beach shark fishing for large sharks can be spotted because fishermen will be using large, conventional-type reels 6/O–9/O (6 ought–9 ought) or larger in size.

3. Fishing piers—due to structure, constant bait in the water, struggling fish throughout the day and night, and cleaning tables that let fish entrails back into the ocean—are areas that are attractive to sharks. Warnings stating "No Swimming, Wading, or Surfing Within 300–500 Feet of a Pier" should be put in place and enforced as a safety precaution to water users.

4. Educate the public through the distribution of informational brochures which detail how to reduce one's risk of encountering a shark. A list of suggestions was given to town officials.

The significant injuries sustained by the victims, the depth of water where the attacks took place, and the bump-and-bite type of attack that both victims described all point to a bull shark as the most likely species involved in these 2015 cases. The bites occurred within two miles of one another, and the two incidents occurred less than ninety minutes apart. On three different occasions that day, a helicopter patrolman spotted sharks that were dark in color and approximately seven feet long; officials believe that all three sightings were of the same shark. It is also possible that the same shark (spotted by the helicopter patrolman three different times on the same day) was also involved in both attacks earlier in the day. This would be an extremely rare event if proven true. I believe it is more likely that several species of sharks, including larger bull sharks, were feeding on schools of fish running through the area and that two different bull sharks were involved in the two attacks. Both incidents were a rare misfortune for the victims. These two individuals were in the water at the wrong place and at the wrong time—a time when large predators were present, hunting the surf zone. During that same year, all along the North Carolina coast, piers were reporting catches of large red drum (a species of game fish). This was something that hadn't been seen since the 1960s. Usually, fishermen found the red drum species farther from shore. This was another clue indicating unusual fish migration patterns for 2015.

The GSAF records indicate that Oak Island had never before had an official recorded shark attack off its beaches. We have records dating back from 1853 to the present for North Carolina. Bites have occurred at Holden Beach, Ocean Isle Beach, and Bald Head Island in Brunswick County, but the 2015 cases were the first ever recorded for Oak Island, North Carolina.

Additional Cases Likely Involving the Big Three

North and South Carolina have cases of several shark-related human deaths in which the shark species involved is not identified. Even though positive identification of attacking shark species can be difficult to determine, cases involving serious injuries and fatalities usually, more times than not, point to one of the deadly trio. Whether each of the following cases involved death due to shark attack or whether the shark involvement was postmortem, the likely culprits in each case included white sharks, tiger sharks, or bull sharks. But this is not to say that other species which have occasionally killed a person could not have been involved.

"Off the Battery" in South Carolina, 1853 or 1854: A young man's boat was capsized off a place referred to as "the Battery" (perhaps in Charleston). The man capsized while trying to fight off a shark that had been following his boat. The man disappeared and was never seen again. Months later, his gold watch was found inside a shark's stomach. It is unknown whether the victim drowned prior to death or whether a shark killed him. (Case #GSAF 1853.00.00b)

South Carolina, 1883: A steamboat crew positioned off the coast of South Carolina saw a descending balloon carrying a person. Crew members reported that the balloonist failed at an attempted landing, came across the beach, and was dragged over the water. A school of sharks leaped out of the water with great splashing and caught the aeronaut. White sharks and bull sharks, among other species, have been known to attack and share a single prey target in pairs or more. Documented reports also show that two different shark species have been involved in a simultaneous attack. (Case #GSAF 1883.00.00a)

Ocracoke, North Carolina, between 1900 and 1905: A shark killed a U.S. Coast Guardsman who was swimming at Ocracoke. No further information is available on the incident. (Case #GSAF ND.0003)

Ocracoke, North Carolina, July 1905: A fisherman who was said to be a Coast Guardsman was fishing for red drum across the Pamlico Sound at Ocracoke, North Carolina, when he was killed by a shark. No further details are available on this incident; however, given the severity of the attack, the location of the attack in a sound, and speculation that the man was likely fishing in the surf while standing in shallow water, a bull shark is the most likely species to have been involved. (Case #GSAF 1905.07.00)

Charleston, South Carolina, July 12, 1913: The GSAF lists a fatal shark attack on a soldier. No further details are available on this attack. (Case #GSAF 1913.07.12)

Parris Island Marine Corps Recruit Depot, Beaufort County, South Carolina, August 1960: Reports state that a shark devoured a young U.S. Marine Corps (USMC) recruit stationed at Parris Island as the man was attempting to swim to shore to allegedly escape cruel treatment by ranking superiors on the island. Senator Styles Bridges was informed of this incident, and he got in touch with General David M. Shoop and USMC Parris Island authorities, who began conducting a full investigation into the matter. Victor M. Coppleson lists this incident in the 1962 edition of his book, *Shark Attack*,[54] and a *Miami News* article reported on the attack in the August 3, 1960, issue.[55] I contacted officials at Parris Island years ago seeking additional information on this case but could not gather any further data. Such a severe attack, if valid, would have most assuredly been the work of a white shark, tiger, or bull shark. (Case #GSAF 1960.08.00)

Atlantic Beach, North Carolina, June 2, 2019: Seventeen-year-old Paige Winter was standing in waist-deep water with her sister and brother enjoying the afternoon sun and surf. At approximately noon, Paige's father, Charlie Winter, who was in the water with his children, had just turned his back when he heard someone scream his name. Turning around, Charlie witnessed Paige yelling to him as she vanished beneath the water. At first, Paige thought one of her siblings was grabbing her leg as a joke, but then she started feeling a "snapping" sensation as the animal started shaking her—similar to what a dog would do when playing with a toy rope. For a second, while underwater, Paige recalls giving up as her body went into shock, and she remembers eventually not feeling any pain. Mustering all her strength, she tried to pry the shark off, but it was too strong. Her father, rushing as fast as he could to her rescue, saw a pinkish material gathering where his daughter disappeared as he dove in at a depth of approximately five feet of water to find her. Within seconds, Charlie found himself staring eye-to-eye with a shark that was later estimated to have been around eight feet long. He pulled his daughter up and witnessed the shark's head as it came up with her, attached to her left leg. Charlie immediately began hitting the shark with all the strength he had. According to Charlie, "He was just staring at me sideways, just the biggest, blackest eye piercing. It was just no negotiating with it." The shark finally let go of Paige, and Charlie grabbed her by her upper body, placed her over his shoulder, and brought her back to shore—with the shark following from behind. Charlie fell to the sand in exhaustion as others then took Paige up onto the beach. People began bringing anything they could think of that might be able to stop her bleeding. One man happened to pass by, wearing a belt that he offered to Charlie, who made a tourniquet around Paige's leg. That belt ended up helping to save her life. Paige was airlifted to Vidant Trauma Center in Greenville, North Carolina, where surgeons worked to successfully save her. Paige suffered deep lacerations to her left leg, pelvis, and hands, requiring a blood transfusion upon arrival. The major artery and vein supplying blood to the left leg were severed. Surgeons amputated her left leg at the thigh and her fourth and fifth fingers on her left hand due to the severity of the wounds. Dr. Richard Zeri, a plastic surgeon at Vidant Medical Center, stated, "The bites resulted in some extensive tissue damage, and the wounds were almost surgical. The shark's teeth were extremely sharp. It looks like there was a knife taken to her injuries." According to Dr. Eric A. Toschlog, Chief of Trauma at Vidant Medical Center, "I've had some experience with shark attack victims before, and based on what I know, I think it was a Bull Shark. [. . .] We can't confirm it yet, but that would be my opinion." He added that the attack on Paige and the devastation of her wounds were the worst shark-related injuries he had seen or treated since a series of attacks in 2001 off the Outer Banks of North Carolina. (Case #GSAF 2019.06.02)

In my role as an investigator for the SRI, I was able to reach Paige's father not long after this incident occurred; however, as of this writing, I have been unable to get the pertinent information needed for positive species identification of the shark involved. In my opinion, the evidence discovered in this case certainly points to one of the big three; though it is very possible that a bull shark, as experts have theorized, was not the attacking species. Consider the following evidence:

Description of the wounds: Although the wound descriptions in this case lack specific detail, Dr. Zeri's statement that "the wounds were almost surgical" in my experience points to the tiger shark. Because of their unique, sharp-cutting teeth of equal size in the upper and lower jaws, tiger sharks leave sawlike wound patterns on the upper and lower sections of a bite. These injuries lack puncture wounds caused by the lower jaw–holding teeth of other species, such as the bull shark. To be more certain regarding Paige Winter's case, however, investigators would have had to gather clear preoperative wound photos and send them to an expert for scientific bite-wound analysis.

Behavior of the shark during the attack: Paige Winter's attack is similar to the following incident involving a tiger shark, specifically in the way that both animals latched on to their victims and remained attached until rescuers finally pressured them enough to release their victims:

On Sunday, July 27, 1958, twelve-year-old Douglas Lawton was swimming with his brother in the Gulf of Mexico in Sarasota, Florida. Diving underneath for seashells, Douglas suddenly started screaming. Pulled off his feet, he almost went completely under as the water surface began turning red. When Douglas's brother grabbed him and held his head up, people saw the shark for the first time; he was striking Douglas's leg. Four adults (including Douglas's uncle) rushed into the water and started pulling the boy out. They witnessed the shark still clinging to the inner surface of the boy's thigh. Douglas tried to dislodge the shark's head with his left hand as his uncle held Douglas by his shoulders and his father grabbed the shark's tail until it released his son. The shark floundered back from the very shallow water adjacent to the shore, entered deeper water, and swam away. Douglas was then rushed to the hospital for successful emergency treatment. Based on witnesses' descriptions of the shark and based on the wound characteristics, investigators identified the attacking species as a young tiger shark about five or six feet long. (Case #GSAF 1958.07.27b)

Description of the shark: Charlie Winter (Paige's father) saw the animal, and his documented description states that the shark had "the biggest, blackest eye." Bull sharks characteristically have small, beady eyes that are not black in color. But tiger sharks and white sharks have large, jet-black eyes. This crucial piece of evidence seems to rule out a bull shark as the attacking species. A white shark cannot be ruled out as the attacking species in Paige Winter's case. Consider the following incident—this time noticing the similar descriptions of the sharks' behaviors:

On Sunday, February 27, 1966, thirteen-year-old Raymond Short was swimming in New South Wales, Australia, when he felt a nudge on his left leg, glanced down, and saw the shark. "It shook my leg then let it go and swam around me in a circle," he said. "I wondered why there was no pain. I could see the blood; the water was turning pink. It hit me again, another bump just like the first, only this time on the right leg. My whole body seemed numb from the waist down. I thought: 'The shore. If only I could reach the shore, I could make it.' Suddenly I was lifted up out of the water. The shark had my whole leg in its mouth, its jaws just over my knee." Ray tried to gouge the shark's eye and then bit the shark very hard on its snout. "Its nose was like hard, old, salty canvas," he recalled. The bite had no effect on the shark. "Then, my right foot felt something hard. Now I was standing on one leg. I had been washed onto a sandbank," he recalled. The shark stopped moving but was still attached to Ray's leg. Rescuers arrived and told the boy that the shark had gone, but he kept insisting, "It's still there!" Then, one rescuer discovered that the shark had been hidden in the bloody water as they carried the boy (and, unbeknownst to them, the shark that was still attached to his leg) onto the beach. They beat the shark with sticks and a surfboard, but only when one man fetched a rifle and hit it on the head did the shark relax his grip on the boy's leg so that Ray could be transferred to the hospital for successful treatment. In examining the shark on the following day, investigators found massive abdominal wounds of recent origin on the left and right lower abdominal surfaces and on the dorsal and ventral region between the pelvic and caudal fins. Investigators also noted multiple lacerations and parallel scratch marks across the entire above region. One wound on the ventral surface was elliptical in shape, each half forming the typical parabolic curves of the upper and lower jaws of another shark. The dimensions indicated that the attacking shark was approximately the same size as its victimized shark. One wound penetrated the abdominal cavity. Stomach content analysis revealed two pieces of undigested squid and several dozen fish vertebrae. The shark that attacked Raymond was identified as a 2.5-metre (8'3") immature female white shark. (Case #GSAF 1966.02.27)

....

The shark that attacked Paige Winter—no matter the species—could have also been suffering from wounds that were preventing it from capturing prey in a typical fashion. Charlie Winter had successfully tried hitting the animal numerous times. Normally, when attacked, a shark's instinct is to shield its eyes with a nictitating membrane or, as with a white shark, roll its eyes back as a form of eye protection. In either case, a witness should be seeing an eye appearing closed (nictitating membrane) or a large, white eye (eyes rolled back for protection). Charlie describes seeing only a large, black eye. This doesn't mean that the shark didn't instinctively protect its eyes, but if it did not—*and* if the eyes remained black as Charlie was assaulting it—it does suggest that there could have been something wrong with the animal in Paige Winter's case.

The shark could have endured injuries from another animal prior to its attack on Paige, similar to those noted on the white shark in the Raymond Short case. Other possibilities include internal damage from swallowing a hook or injuries sustained from a boat propellor, or it could have been sick.

5 Cause of Death in Coastal Waters of the Carolinas

Sometimes, unknown-cause-of-death cases are dismissed as ocean-related drownings, even when evidence exists of a potential shark attack. A documented drowning conclusion, where there is evidence of possible shark involvement prior to death, not only skews shark attack statistics but also can inaccurately inform the public in terms of actual cause of death. Cases where cause of death is undetermined but include evidence of shark involvement at some point should be documented and labeled as "shark attack prior to death not ruled out or confirmed (SAPTDU)," as I have done in this book and as is done in the Global Shark Attack File. The database should not include these cases in confirmed shark attack numbers, but neither should they be discarded and not listed as possible additional cases.

Death from drowning should also not be the easy scapegoat for questionable ocean deaths that it seems to be. According to Michael H. A. Piette and Dr. Els A. De Letter, "Death by drowning remains one of the most difficult diagnoses in forensic medicine. To demonstrate drowning unambiguously as the cause of death remains a difficult issue in current forensic practice. The ideal diagnostic test as definite proof for drowning still needs to be established. To ascribe drowning as a cause of death to a body found in water without some evidence of the effect of having aspirated water is risky. It may be more accurate to list a differential diagnosis rather than a specific cause of death. Police information such as eye witnessing, as an example, can be much more reliable."[1]

The following additional Carolina incidents are likely excluded by other research organizations because death from shark attack was not positively confirmed. They are listed here because the incident did involve a shark at some point and cause of death is unknown.

South Carolina, 1837: Part of a man's body, which was still clothed with a portion of his sailor's uniform, was recovered from a large shark's stomach. The shark was caught on hook and line off of the "Southern Wharf" and was said to have been twenty-five feet long. Shark involvement prior to death, in this case, has not been confirmed or ruled out. The recorded size of the animal that contained the human remains is likely inaccurate, but it was undoubtedly either a white shark or a tiger shark. (Case #GSAF 1837.00.00a)

Elizabeth City, Pasquotank County, North Carolina, September 5, 1881: The body of Frank G. Hines of Edenton, North Carolina, was found washed up on a beach at Elizabeth City. According to the *Elizabeth City Economist,* Hines's body was found on a Monday morning a mile and a half below the place where he drowned. The article also states that the general impression was that Hines was struck by a shark while bathing in the surf. Death due to shark bite is not ruled out or confirmed in this case. (Case #GSAF 1881.09.05)

Bulls Bay, near Charleston, South Carolina, 1883: A man's body was recovered in Bulls Bay. His arm was reported to have been bitten off by a shark. The man likely drowned prior to being bitten; however, death from shark attack cannot be ruled out. The lost limb highly points to one of the big three. (Case #GSAF 1883.00.00b)

Missing Persons and Shark Attacks

What about cases where a swimmer, diver, or surfer vanishes suddenly and quickly, and the body is never found? In most cases such as these, investigators conclude that drowning was the likely cause of death. This may be the case in many of these incidents, or even most of them; however, there are cases of this nature that support evidence of shark involvement, and any honest analysis from an unbiased investigation into such incidents should not rule out the possibility of shark attack as the cause of death unless concrete evidence proves otherwise. Most shark attack experts document this type of fatal shark attack—where a victim is taken, never to be seen again—only if people witnessed the attack. Any other person who has gone missing from the ocean and who is never found is usually labeled as a drowning death. As mentioned in the last section, drowning shouldn't be assumed when cause of death is unknown and especially if shark involvement is a possibility. I believe that ignoring these types of cases when studying shark attack data leads to inaccurate and misleading statistics for the public. I only include incidents of a missing person or a body found in the collected data for the Shark Research Institute if there is some connection to shark involvement, but I do pay close attention to any incident I hear of when a body is never found—as in the following incident. It is highly unusual for a body not to be recovered in cases of actual drowning.

According to Wrightsville Beach Police Chief Dan House—in an article from the *Wilmington Star-News*—in winter months, when water temperatures can dip to the forties and fifties, a body can stay submerged for more than a week. But when water temperatures reach the mid-eighties, a drowned body should surface much quicker. The article continues:

> When someone drowns, they typically sink immediately, which results in the victim going down at the point he or she was last seen on the surface, said Sgt. Steven Schmidlin, commander of the New Hanover County Sheriff's Office Marine Unit. The currents at the bottom are not nearly as active as on the surface and little if any movement happens at that time, he explained.
>
> "My experience is—once a person goes down in the water, we will find them in less than 50 feet of where they went in," he said.
>
> When the body resurfaces—in warmer temperatures within about four days—it will come up not far from where it disappeared and be carried elsewhere by surface currents, he said.
>
> "The warmer the water, the quicker they'll rise," Schmidlin said.[2]

This article revolves around a swimmer named Chuck Kuebler who went missing off Wrightsville Beach on July 26, 2016. Investigators never found his body, and authorities continue to treat this incident as a missing person case. According to the article each summer, when the water was warm like it was in late July 2016, Chuck Kuebler practiced swimming the more-than-one-mile distance between Johnnie Mercers Fishing Pier and Crystal Pier. The day before Chuck went missing, Wrightsville Beach Ocean Rescue members had brought him back to shore. He had been swimming out past the breakers, a lot farther out than most people would venture. The crew that brought him in stated that he seemed fine and was not in any type of distress. "That contact added to the puzzle of Kuebler's whereabouts," the article says, before quoting Chief House: "Every expert that I've talked to said it's more likely than not that by now something should have come up [. . . But] that's not always 100 percent true. . . . Maybe if the currents were right and the tides were right, they could have swept him out and he's gone forever [. . .] but he should have surfaced by now. Even the fishermen agree with that." Chief House said that his office would continue land and shore searches, including areas where Coast Guard calculations indicate currents would have carried a body. "Until we have a body, or we find him somewhere alive, the case will stay open."[3]

What actually happened to Chuck Kuebler? No one knows because he is still missing. Investigators have found no evidence of shark involvement in his case and no confirmation that he drowned. If the outcome of this incident were different, and evidence supported possible shark attack, I would have submitted the case for inclusion into the GSAF, labeled as "shark attack prior to death not ruled out or confirmed (SAPTDU)." Other research organizations would most certainly disregard such cases regardless of evidence of shark involvement, as can be seen by comparing their shark attack statistics with those of the the GSAF databank.

The following missing person cases, possibly involving shark attack prior to death, have occurred in Carolina waters.

Charleston Harbor, Charleston County, South Carolina, 1847: A young sailor who said he was not afraid of sharks undertook a swim to Castle Pinckney, a large marshy island located on Shutes Folly. His goal was to swim to the island and then back to the wharf in Charleston Harbor. It's recorded that during his swim, he suddenly disappeared. He was thought to have been taken by a shark. Even though there is no further evidence that he was killed by a shark, he did vanish suddenly, without struggle, and it appears that his body was never found. Shark involvement was suspected then, so I don't rule it out now. (Case #GSAF 1847.00.00b)

Off Cape Lookout Shoal, North Carolina, May 31, 1992: Forty-five-year-old Mike Weathers and seven others were diving and exploring the wreck of the German submarine *U-352*, located twenty-six miles south of Morehead City, North Carolina, in 125 feet of water. When the other divers returned to the surface, Mike decided to go back down. He never returned. His heavy nylon diving vest, complete with his name tag, was found torn near the shoulder. At the site where he disappeared, divers discovered an air tank, a regulator, a mouthpiece, and a dive computer with Mike's name on them. Additionally divers also found other equipment believed to have belonged to him. Although some experts believe that sharks may have torn the vest, U.S. Coast Guard investigators stated that there was no evidence of a shark attack. Therefore, the official report stated that he likely drowned and that the vest was torn postmortem. Others theorize that Weathers was the victim of a shark attack. (Case #GSAF 1992.05.31)

Because I cannot agree with the Coast Guard investigators' statement that the body showed no evidence of a shark attack, I have documented this case as "shark attack prior to death not ruled out or confirmed (SAPTDU)." This listing does not eliminate the drowning theory, nor does it deny the unmistakable evidence—in light of the torn diving vest—of shark involvement at some point, either prior to death or postmortem. Consider similarities among the following cases from different locations as further evidence pointing to possible shark attack as the cause of death in the Mike Weathers incident.

On the night of September 13, 1995, twenty-five-year-old William Covert was with four friends diving to collect marine fish when he disappeared. They were anchored a few miles off Alligator Reef Light near Islamorada in the Florida Keys, Monroe County, looking for fish on a reef. He was using scuba gear, whereas the others were using hookah gear with thirty-foot hoses connected to the twenty-two-foot boat from which they were diving. The last time William was seen—about forty-five minutes into the dive—was when one of the other divers saw him attempting to catch fish on the edge of the reef wall. Not long after he was last seen, Tom Scaturro, the owner of the boat, became concerned about Williams' air supply and dive time, so he entered the water to check on William. He found William's air tank, pail, and netting on the bottom of the sea floor, but there was no sign of William. Tom and the rest of the dive team continued looking for William but to no avail. Soon, the Coast Guard, the Marine Patrol, the Monroe County Sheriff's Department, and the Key Largo Volunteer Fire Department arrived to assist in the search. Some of William's friends from Michigan even flew in to help. Eventually searchers recovered additional items belonging to William. Total recovery included an air tank containing an ample amount of air, a regulator, shredded blue BVDs, a white T-shirt that was jaggedly torn from the bottom, sweatpants pierced by thumb-sized holes, a diver's face mask, eleven pounds of dive weights, and the weight belt. Divers recovered these remains in thirty-five feet of water around four miles southwest of Alligator Reef Light.

During many hours of analysis, in an attempt to determine what happened to William, shark experts studied the remains of his T-shirt and sweatpants, comparing shark jaws from several species to the tears in the clothing. According to Dr. Gordon Hubbell of the GSAF, "I was able to match the bite marks on the dive belt and T-shirt" to those made by a bull shark in the size range of ten feet to twelve feet in length. "The radius of all the bites match," added Dr. Jose Castro of the Mote Marine Laboratory (MML) in Sarasota, Florida. They concluded that the 5'5", 170-pound diver was killed and consumed by a bull shark. Investigators think that William likely confronted the shark and shed the tank to escape to the surface. The shark bite marks on the T-shirt indicate that William may have lost an arm during his escape attempt. "The top had the marks of the upper teeth on the upper surface of the shirt sleeve," and puncture marks were present on the bottom surface of the shirt. Investigators believe that William may have lost his other arm while fending off the animal. The shark also bit into his abdomen, tearing a half-moon-shaped chunk from his nylon dive belt.

Other shark experts believe that the evidence in William's case does not conclusively support the shark attack scenario, stating that he could have drowned first and been scavenged postmortem. (Case #GSAF 1995.09.13)

On September 9, 1987, diver Terrance Gibson, forty-seven years old, vanished and was never found again. He had been diving alone for scallops at Marino Rocks in South Australia. The only items of Terry's that divers recovered were an air tank, one diving boot, a buoyancy vest, and a dive belt. The belt bore teeth marks of a white shark on its weights. (Case #GSAF 1987.09.08)

On September 8, 1991, nineteen-year-old Jonathon Lee was scuba diving off Snapper Point at Aldinga Beach, South Australia, when he was taken by a white shark. His diving partner, Dave Roberts, said that the shark flashed past him, shaking its head from side to side. The shark had Jonathan in its mouth, and there was nothing that Roberts could do. Two other divers in the water tried to locate Jonathan, but they found only a scuba tank, a severed air hose, two swim fins, and other pieces of diving equipment. Police officials found only a small part of Jonathan's body later that day. (Case #GSAF 1991.09.08)

March 8, 1992, diver Kazuta Harada, forty-one years old, was was collecting pen shells offshore of Matsuyama, Ehime Prefecture,

Japan, when he was attacked by a large white shark. Divers recovered only a helmet and a severely damaged diving suit, which was missing its right side and right leg. His body was never found.[4] (Case #GSAF 1992.03.08 c)

On June 5, 1993, thirty-five-year-old Therese Cartwright was diving with her husband, Ian, off Tenth Island, on Tasmania's northeastern coast. They were about five meters (about sixteen feet) deep when a large white shark came from behind and took Therese in its massive jaws in a matter of seconds. Later that afternoon divers recovered only her leg, which was still within its wetsuit material. (Case #GSAF 1993.06.05)

The following two Carolina cases also did not make it into other shark attack research data. Both cases resemble the disappearance of Chuck Kuebler off Wrightsville Beach, North Carolina (discussed earlier in this chapter); however, both of these cases do include evidence of shark involvement.

On September 11, 2005, at Folly Beach, Charleston County, South Carolina, eighteen-year-old Greg Allen Norton Jr. was surfing with several friends about two hundred feet from shore. Waves that day were about three to four feet during high tide. At around 2:00 p.m., Greg was in the water and not attached to his surfboard when he vanished without a sound. Witnesses said that he was there one moment and gone the next. After he vanished, his friends saw only his surfboard floating on the water. Two witnesses said that they had spotted sharks in the area at the time the surfer disappeared and that perhaps one of the sharks had pulled him under the water. Alton Wiggins stated that he spoke with a friend of Greg's who was nearby when he disappeared. This witness told Wiggins that he had watched a shark hit a nearby surfer and then pull him underwater. Another witness said that sharks had been spotted swimming in the area where Greg had been. Others reported seeing porpoises. Greg's recovered surfboard showed no signs of a shark bite, and authorities treated the incident as a search for a missing surfer—not a shark attack.

Greg Allen Norton Jr. was never found. Because I believe that the evidence cannot definitively rule out the possibility of a fatal shark attack, GSAF has placed this case in the "shark attack prior to death not ruled out or confirmed (SAPTDU)" category. It is unusual for a body to never be found, and the circumstances surrounding Greg's disappearance are very odd: He vanished without a sound, without a splash, without any signs of struggle, and without the slightest call for help. As mentioned, several witnesses stated that sharks were swimming in the area at the time the teenager vanished.[5] (Case #GSAF 2005.09.11)

On July 12, 2014, another unusual Folly Beach case—similar to the Greg Norton incident—occurred. That Saturday afternoon around 2:00 p.m., nineteen-year-old Tristen Allen and his father took their twenty-two-foot Carolina skiff out for a short thirty-minute dive thirteen miles southeast of South Carolina's Folly Beach. They were diving in water approximately sixty feet deep. According to Tristen's father, they left the sea bottom together, holding hands, until they reached the surface. While on the surface, Tristen's father witnessed his son disappear—quickly and without a sound—beneath the water. Tristen seemed to have been struggling to remove his gear as he vanished. He was gone in an instant and was nowhere to be found, even after his father and others dove for hours trying to locate him. Approximately two weeks later, divers recovered bone fragments from an area known as the Charleston 60 Reef, near where Tristen and his father had been diving. Forensic experts tested the remains and determined that they were Tristen's. Authorities have not released any further information as to the speculated cause of death. The official cause of death in this case is unknown, but I find the circumstances surrounding this incident to be suspicious. Tristen suddenly, and without a sound, vanished right in front of his father, and the father could not find a trace of his son—even though Tristen had been right there with him moments before. Even after spending hours diving and searching, the father never found his son's remains. Not until two weeks later did divers recover bone fragments that they later determined to be from Tristen's body. The evidence makes an obvious case that one or several sharks were involved at some point between when Tristen disappeared and when divers found his remains.[6]

Officials initially announced to the public that Tristen's body "had been found." It wasn't until the family's spokesperson requested that authorities revise the official statement to to "his *remains* were found"[7]—a more accurate account—that the public gained this knowledge. Had officials not clarified their original statement, an important piece to this investigation would have remained hidden. I am not suggesting that Tristen was a shark attack victim; as an investigator, however, I cannot say for certain that he wasn't. Because of the quick and suspicious way in which the diver vanished in front of his father and could not be located by divers after hours of searching—and yet his remains *were* later found—I have listed this this case as "shark attack prior to death not ruled out or confirmed."

Although I may not agree with the philosophy and attitude of shark hunter Vic Hislop toward white sharks, tiger sharks, and other dangerous species, and although I dislike the slaughter he has perpetrated against hundreds of sharks, I do believe that Hislop's book *Shark Man* includes some valid points and interesting statistics, especially regarding missing persons and shark attacks. According to Hislop, most eyewitnessed shark attacks come from what he considers to be "small" sharks—in the nine- to fourteen-foot range. These sharks grab a person, and the victim may even lose an arm or a leg during the struggle. Hislop also claims that far *more* cases of shark attacks actually occur from larger animals—those capable of snatching an entire person from the surface all at once, sometimes without leaving a visible trace of blood, as the shark swallows its prey whole, or takes it to deeper water to be consumed. Their victims are then passed off mistakenly as missing persons due to drowning. Hislop has observed his home area of Moreton Bay in Queensland, Australia, and asserts that he has lost count of the number of people who have vanished there. He also had a survey conducted in the Phillip Island, Victoria, area of Australia—where former Prime

Minister Harold Holt suddenly disappeared while swimming at Cheviot Beach near Portsea, Victoria, on December 17, 1967. His body was never found. Hislop discovered that 119 people had gone missing in that same area in a period of seventeen-and-a-half years following the prime minister's disappearance. In his book, Hislop adds that sometimes incidents have occurred in which authorities later find a body *part* and officially state to the public that they have found a *body* (similar to how things transpired in the 2014 Tristen Allen incident). Hislop certainly doesn't claim that all of these missing persons were shark attack victims, but he does believe that there are far more attacks from animals that leave no trace or evidence than authorities officially document. Hislop has also personally recorded some shark attacks in the same area in which he conducted his research, and one case in particular—mentioned in his book— bears some similarities to the Folly Beach, South Carolina, vanishings of Greg Allen Norton Jr. (2005) and Tristen Allen (2014).

According to Hislop, in the Victoria area that he had surveyed, five lifeguards had been swimming in the water simultaneously. The captain of the Surrento Surf Club was one of them. The captain and one other lifesaver were talking and treading water just outside the surf break. They were about three feet apart when the captain claims that, as he and his friend were talking, a large shark's nose appeared beside the friend and took him by the head and body. He said he could hear his friend's bones breaking as the shark shut its mouth. The captain heard no splash, no scream, just nothing—it was almost as if his friend had never existed. He was just . . . gone. If this *is* a confirmed shark attack case, then it does give some weight to Vic Hislop's opinion on what he believes has happened to at least some of the missing persons in the geographic area on which his survey had focused.

Perhaps these rare attacks represent a different hunting method of large sharks and we should document them as a separate type of shark attack, or maybe we should label these underwater—almost "silent"—assaults as a subcategory of sneak attacks. Notice with each of the following cases *how* the sharks take their victims—in particular, how these cases differ from the sneak attacks mentioned earlier, where sharks were seen breaching the water and taking their victims violently in one swoop of splashing commotion. Instead, victims in the following cases are taken without warning, without much sound, and with no indication of a typical shark sneak attack. As you'll see, these victims are snatched by the animal at the surface or from underneath the water in an instant, sometimes without any hint that a shark is present. I use these tragic cases on record as evidence to support the possibility of shark attacks regarding the Greg Allen Norton Jr. and Tristen Allen incidents. Consider the following:

On July 21, 1897, a young boy was beaching caught fish from a seine net in the Indian Ocean at Back Beach, Durban, Kwa-Zulu-Natal, South Africa. Some of the catch had escaped the nets, and the boy had waded out to retrieve the fish. He was standing in shallow water when a shark appeared and dragged the boy under the water instantaneously. No trace of him was ever found. (Case #GSAF 1897.07.21)

On January 8, 1908, a Japanese fisherman was swimming in the water off Mana, Kauai, Hawaii, gathering fish that had been killed with dynamite. Someone nearby gave warning that a shark was in the area, so the fisherman began swimming vigorously for safety toward some nearby rocks; however, before he could reach the rocks, something grabbed him and pulled him under the water. He was last seen with his arms around the animal's body before he vanished for good. (Case #GSAF 1908.01.08)

On May 1, 1911, James Jantjes and a number of people were swimming in the Indian Ocean within Victoria Bay, northeast of Mossel Bay in the Western Cape Province of South Africa. James decided to swim out farther than the rest, against the others' advice. He made it farther out than the others in the group when witnesses stated that he was taken by a shark. James was swimming when suddenly he threw one hand up and vanished beneath the surface, never to be seen again. Some people believe that one contributing factor to this incident was a fishery established at Victoria Bay that had been attracting sharks close inshore for some time. It was reported that witnesses had seen many man-eaters in the area prior to the attack. (Case #GSAF 1911.05.01)

On July 23, 1926, at around 11:00 a.m., twenty-year-old Augusto Casellato was swimming with his friend, Luigi Baldi, toward a cliff called Punta dell'Uomo in the waters in Golfo di Genova of the Ligurian Sea at a resort in Varazze, Italy. The two young men were racing as they swam toward the cliff, with Luigi about ten meters (almost thirty-three feet) ahead of Augusto. About two hundred meters (656 feet) from the cliff, Luigi suddenly heard a stifled cry from behind. He looked around just in time to see his friend, Augusto, struggling furiously in the water right before he quickly disappeared beneath the surface without even managing to wave his arms. Luigi immediately swam toward where his friend had vanished. Just before reaching the spot, he saw the dark tail of a huge shark right below the surface. Some people on a nearby boat also witnessed what happened and headed straight to Luigi, pulling him out of the water as fast as they could. Lifeboats soon arrived in the area where Augusto had vanished, and divers began searching for the swimmer. The only items they ever recovered were his bathing suit and cap on the following day. (Case #GSAF 1926.07.23)

On April 1, 1934, a young boy swimming in the Indian Ocean at Granny's Pool—near Castle Rock Corner, Winkelspruit, South Africa—got caught in a rip current and was taken seaward. Lifeguard Neville Doveton went to the boy's rescue. Wearing belt rescue equipment, he was taking a line out to save the distressed swimmer. When he was about sixteen feet from the boy, the lifeguard heard him suddenly scream and then saw him disappearing beneath the water. A line of witnesses along the nearby rocks began shouting that a shark had taken the boy. They signaled the lifeguards on the beach to quickly reel Doveton back to shore. As he was being pulled back, the lifeguard felt something brush against his legs. The young swimmer who had vanished in the surf was never seen again. (Case #GSAF 1934.04.01c)

On December 27, 1938, nineteen-year-old Daniel Graham was surfing at North Beach—at the mouth of the Bellinger River—in northern New South Wales, Australia, when he suddenly and swiftly disappeared beneath the water. Other surfers saw him throw up his hands and vanish. Local law enforcement organized various search patrols but never found a trace of him. Surfers who were with Daniel and witnessed the disappearance said that he appeared to be in no distress when he sank under, and they believe that he was seized by a shark. Because no witnesses saw the shark actually take the surfer, the GSAF lists this case as "shark attack prior to death not ruled out or confirmed (SAPTDU)." (Case #GSAF 1938.12.27)

On May 3, 1939, British freighter *Huncliffe* was several hundred miles from shore in the Gulf Stream off Cape Henry, Virginia, when a rogue wave crashed over the bow and knocked crewmember John Heagan overboard into the sea. John was reported to have been a powerful swimmer, and he was making good progress back toward the ship and to a lifebuoy that crew members had thrown to him. The shipmates were in the process of lowering a lifeboat when they saw sharks in the water, and when John was in range of the ship, he suddenly cried out, threw his hands up, and was pulled beneath the surface, never to be seen again. The crew of the *Huncliffe*—along with two other boats—searched the area for four hours but could not find a trace of John. (Case #GSAF 1939.05.03)

On July 22, 1944, seventeen-year-old Albert Schmidt was swimming in the warm waters of the Indian Ocean at Hartenbos in the Western Cape Province of South Africa. Friends later reported that Albert had a sore on his shin that may have been bleeding that day. Six other people were swimming in the water around him, and one of them said that Albert laughed and said that a shark was at his leg. Albert then swam two or three meters (six-and-a-half feet) and suddenly disappeared. A large amount of blood surfaced and dissipated at the spot where he went under. Witnesses on the shore claimed that they had seen a shark swimming in the swells, and then the animal appeared between Albert and the shore. One person said that they heard Albert shout for help. Witnesses on the beach saw him struggling before he vanished. A boat arrived in the area soon after Albert's disappearance, but his body was never found. (Case #GSAF 1944.07.22)

On August 20, 1944, at the rocks below the Marina Hotel, Margate, South Africa, nineteen-year-old Dennis Nissen decided to ignore a bathing ban that lifeguards had put in place due to dirty water flowing in from the Umzimkulu River. The lifeguards didn't stop him from entering the water, but instead they accompanied Dennis on his swim—one lifeguard on each side of him—in case he got into trouble. As the three swimmers were making their way around a rocky outcrop known locally as The Point, witnesses saw a large shark suddenly grab Dennis by the leg. He screamed once and vanished beneath the waves, never to surface again. (Case #GSAF 1944.08.20)

On January 19, 1975, seventeen-year-old David Barrowman was surfing near Coffin Bay, South Australia. At some point either he fell or something knocked him off his surfboard. As he was swimming to retrieve his surfboard, he disappeared. Three people tried to rescue him, but he was never seen again. One of the rescuers claimed that he heard David yell, "Help! Shark!" before he went under. No witnesses reported a violent struggle or massive splash at the surface; he just vanished. (Case #GSAF 1975.01.19)

On March 11, 1977, offshore of Moreton Bay, Brisbane, Australia, a shark struck two victims, pulling them under to their deaths. Vic Beaver, Verdon Harrison, and John Hayes went for a night fishing trip in the bay when a ship struck their vessel, sinking it and forcing the three men into the black water.

The three men grabbed hold of an icebox and drifted in the current all night and the entire next day. At about 4:30 a.m., near dawn, a large shark appeared and began showing interest in the three men. The shark stuck Vic and disappeared with him. It soon returned, circling beneath the two survivors, eventually grabbing John from underneath the water. It took him by the foot and pulled him under in an instant. John was never seen again. Several hours later Verdon was picked up by a charter fishing vessel. He lived to tell exactly what happened to his friends. Verdon described the animal as the largest shark he had ever seen. It was thought to have been a white shark or a tiger shark. (Cases #GSAF 1977.03.13a/b/c)

On February 28, 1982, customs officer Geert Talen was snorkeling near Lion Rock, South Cape Bay, Tasmania, not far from a freshwater rivulet. The coastal area nearby tends to be rich with seal colonies and frequented by white sharks, with sightings dating back to the days of colonial bay whaling. At approximately 11:00 a.m., as Talen was about ten meters (or thirty-five feet) from shore in calm water, several of his friends witnessed a huge dark shape appear and snatch Geert from the surface. In an instant, Geert was gone, never to be seen again. The predator was so large and black in color that investigators thought it had to have been an orca, but experienced abalone divers who had been close by stated that no killer whales frequented the area during that time of year. The divers headed to the site of the attack and began searching for the missing man; they found only Geert's hand spear on the bottom of the seafloor. They marked the area with a buoy, and soon after, they viewed a huge shark 18 feet in length. It was heavily scarred and had a white rectangular scar within 18 inches of its tail—a big white patch. The shark matched the description of the shark encountered by abalone diver Ray Johnson two weeks earlier at Whale Head 10 kilometers from South Cape Rivulet. From the witnesses' description of the shark and because there has never been a documented case in the wild of an orca attacking and consuming a human, officials determined that a giant white shark had consumed Geert Talen. (Case #GSAF 1982.02.28)

On April 8, 1990, Robert Bullen was diving with three others hunting trochus shells at Dingo Reef, Queensland, Australia, when he suddenly disappeared. Robert was standing on the reef in full view, adjusting his goggles in preparation for his swim back to their anchored dinghy positioned about 30 meters (98 feet) away. Terry Finch, one of the other three divers, claims that he didn't see what happened to Robert but heard a voice, and when he looked around, Robert was gone— nowhere to be found. Robert was an experienced diver and knew to signal if he was in trouble; however, he gave no indication that he was in distress—no call for help, no splashing— he was just standing there one second and was gone the next. Authorities conducted an extensive four-hour search for Robert, but no sign of him was ever found. Divers saw no sharks during the search, but big sharks were said to be common in that area. Terry had no doubt that his friend was taken by a shark, possibly a large tiger shark. (Case #GSAF 1990.04.08)

Perhaps Greg Allen Norton Jr. and Tristen Allen also became victims of a white shark or tiger shark large enough to take them from beneath the surface so easily as to not make even a ripple. Evidence certainly suggests that possibility. With these additional cases bearing such similarities to the Carolina incidents, just imagine what the determining outcomes would have been in each of these other incidents had no witnesses been present. Judging from my experience and research, investigators in each of these fatalities would almost certainly have reported the cause of death as drowning. Who's to say what actually happened to swimmers, divers, or surfers who disappeared in the surf over the years throughout the world, including those in North and South Carolina? Perhaps some of them also fell victim to the jaws of a giant. Without any witnesses to confirm what happened, we may never know for sure. One thing is for certain: When someone vanishes in the ocean and is never found again, we should not rule out shark involvement if the evidence points to that possibility. Cases such as these could be windows into further study of large sharks' rare predation behavior. For the sake of the family members left behind and for the progress in shark research, genuine analysis—with unbiased scrutiny, without any hidden agenda, and without jumping to preconceived or hurried conclusions—is the only investigative approach that should take place.

6 Other Shark Species Implicated in Carolina Attacks

It is obvious that dramatic attacks from the deadly trio in the shark world are out of the ordinary, are far more serious, and are rarer than the average shark bite incidents that occur in the Carolinas and elsewhere around the world. The following discussion pertains to other shark species that officials have suspected, identified, or reported to have been involved in Carolina shark bite incidents.

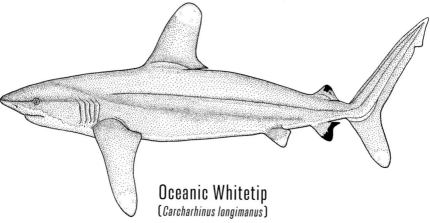

Oceanic Whitetip
(*Carcharhinus longimanus*)

Jacques Cousteau called the oceanic whitetip "the most dangerous of all sharks."[1] This statement could likely be correct if the species were not the nomadic open ocean dwellers that they are. Rarely venturing near shore, these sharks are unlikely to come across humans as often as they encounter other species; thus they are ranked just under the deadly trio as the most dangerous shark to humans. Experts once considered these sharks one of the most abundant large animals on the planet; however, with pelagic fishing operations having greatly reduced their numbers, they are now considered vulnerable. *Oceanic whitetips* are large, thick-bodied sharks with short, flat, rounded snouts. They can reach lengths of thirteen feet and weigh nearly four hundred pounds. Wide, triangular, serrated teeth line the mouth in the upper jaw, and narrower, pointed teeth line the mouth in the lower jaw. They have long, broad-based, paddle-like pectoral fins and a distinctive, broad, rounded dorsal fin tipped with a characteristic white patch. The pectoral fins are also usually tipped with white. Their surface color ranges from a gray to a yellowish-brown, with a white or yellow-tinged ventral surface color.

Oceanic whitetips are slow cruisers, constantly roaming the open seas searching for opportunities to feed. Researchers and divers have described them as dangerous, persistent, aggressive, bold sharks, seemly unaffected by sudden loud noises, bullets shot at them, and various defense mechanisms used against them by divers. They seem to lack fear of anything, and observers have noted that they appear dominant over other pelagic species that may be in the same area. Opportunistic feeders, they will take advantage of an easy meal that comes their way because finding food in the open ocean isn't easy. They may not encounter humans as often as other species, but this shark has likely killed more humans than most others, for oceanic whitetips are usually one of the first shark species to arrive at any sea-related disaster. During World Wars I and II, this shark was a deadly presence at the sites of many sunken ships and multiple planes shot down during battle. For example, oceanic whitetips caused the deaths of many crewmen who were stranded at sea after the sinking of USS *Indianapolis* on July 30, 1945. Oceanic whitetips also killed many who survived the sinking of RMS *Nova Scotia* near South Africa on November 28, 1942. There is really no telling how many soldiers of war and others stranded at sea have lost their lives throughout the years to the oceanic whitetip.

In the Carolinas, oceanic whitetips can be found offshore in the open ocean year-round. Authorities have recorded no official attacks for this species in the Carolinas; however, of the many ships and planes that have gone down at sea off the Carolina coasts, many of those stranded at sea, never to return, likely fell victim to these lone predators. The following two examples are highly likely to have involved the species.

....

On November 12, 1937, the 5,815-ton Greek freighter *Tzenny Chandris* was heading for Rotterdam from Morehead City, North Carolina, carrying a cargo of scrap iron. Early the next evening, the ship ran into a nor'easter and sprang a leak during the storm. The *Tzenny Chandris* battled the storm for three days until her cargo shifted. The ship listed wildly as the autumn gale hurled dreadful seas over her stern, flooding the engine room and extinguishing the lights. Water rose in the hold, the pumps ceased operating, and she finally rolled over on her beam and sank about forty miles east of U.S. Lightship Diamond Shoal. All hands scrambled in a haste to get off the ship and into the dark, cold water. Six crew members had managed to launch a lifeboat, and a northbound tanker picked them up after five hours. Other lifeboats that crew members had launched capsized, and the captain and fourteen sailors spent the next thirty-two hours clinging to bobbing bits of debris. During this time in the water, the captain of the sunken *Tzenny Chandris* received a gash on the bridge of his nose when a sailor who was sharing his improvised raft bit him. The sailor had gone mad from drinking salt water. Other survivors reported a horrible scene. The sea, they later said, had suddenly become alive with sharks. Helpless comrades could only look on as sharks tore the bodies of two seamen to bits and pulled a third through his life belt. Churning the water with their feet as sharks slashed at them, the other terror-stricken sailors somehow managed to drive off their tormentors. Days later on Sunday, November 14, Lieutenant A. C. Keller spotted the survivors and the sharks from his naval plane ninety miles east of Kitty Hawk, North Carolina. He alerted the authorities, and they contacted the U.S. Coast Guard. From his plane, the lieutenant dropped smoke bombs and plunged down in dangerous power dives to frighten off the sharks long enough for a Coast Guard Cutter, the USCGC *Mendota*, to reach the scene and pull the exhausted mariners from the waters. The remaining crew was rescued forty miles from the grave of the *Tzenny Chandris*. Of a crew of twenty-eight sailors, seven were lost. (Case #GSAF 1937.11.13)

....

On December 4, 1943, the Cuban freighter *Libertad* was cruising off the coast of Charleston, South Carolina, when it was torpedoed by the German submarine *U-129*. The freighter sank in one minute. Of the forty-three crewmen aboard, seven were killed, and twenty-eight were left clinging to a capsized lifeboat, rafts, and a tattered hatch cover. The survivors floated in the water for about fifty-three hours before a naval vessel rescued them. During those fifty-three hours, ten men became exhausted, dropped off their floating debris, and were taken by sharks. Julio C. de Cabarrocas, a survivor of the disaster, was bitten in the side by a shark as he tired from fighting them off with his hands and feet. Naval physicians who treated him stated that his wound bore teeth marks. (Case #GSAF 1943.12.04)

....

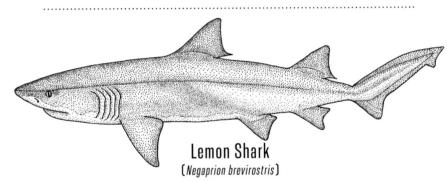

Lemon Shark
(*Negaprion brevirostris*)

In the late 1970s or early 1980s, I was on the end of Springmaid Beach Pier in Myrtle Beach, South Carolina, scanning the sunny water for signs of marine life. It was mid-July, and I was enjoying an annual family vacation at one of my favorite childhood locations. As I was peering into the water, a large recognizable form broke the surface directly in my sights. It was a shark, and it slowly emerged from the depths sideways, its dorsal and ventral sides parallel with the water's surface. When most of its body was on the surface, it righted itself and casually cruised at about a 120-degree angle toward the beach, its dorsal fins and back riding high out of the water.

The first things I noticed about this shark were its size (it was about six feet long), its distinguished yellow color, and its nearly equal-sized first and second dorsal fins. The fin sizes and body color were dead giveaways as to this animal's identity. It was a lemon shark—and the first large shark I had seen swimming in the wild.

Lemon sharks are hefty-bodied bottom dwelling sharks that can reach lengths of eleven feet and can weigh more than four hundred pounds. These sharks carry wide, blunt heads, with teeth in the upper jaws that are narrow and triangular in shape and that lack serrations. The teeth in the lower jaw are also narrow and triangular, with smooth edges along the blade. Lemon sharks are active day and night inshore hunters. They typically hang around docks; cruise the surf zone, saltwater creeks, estuaries, and inlets; and head up rivers into brackish waters searching for food. These sharks may be found in groups and can be aggressive toward humans.

On Thanksgiving Day, November 25, 1976, nineteen-year-old Al Brenneka was surfing at Delray Beach in Palm Beach County, Florida. It was a clear and sunny day, and Al had been in the water for about two hours. He had just ridden a wave to shore and was paddling back out to sea when a shark grabbed his right arm. Al fought the shark as best he could, but the animal managed to bite his arm off below the elbow. Exhausted and bleeding profusely, Al finally floated to the beach. He nearly died from his encounter, and an additional surgical amputation was required above his elbow. Both of his collapsed lungs contained salt water, and he lost the majority of his blood volume. He even went into cardiac arrest twice. He survived his encounter and today is a major advocate for the protection of sharks in the United States. Authorities reported that ten other sharks were in the area at the time of Al's attack. On the basis of a description that Al and other surfers gave to the authorities, experts surmised that a lemon shark about seven feet long attacked him. (Case #GSAF 1976.11.25)

Lemon sharks populate the Carolinas from May through November—and possibly even into December. One was caught in Charleston weighing 317 pounds, and the North Carolina state record lemon shark that weighed 421½ pounds was landed off the Kure Beach Pier in 1978—along with a 390-pounder caught the same year. They can be abundant inshore and do pose a potential threat to swimmers and surfers. Some bites in the Carolinas that are labeled *unknown* for the attacking species could have been the work of lemon sharks, and a couple of cases on file list a lemon shark as the attacking species.

On July 21, 1924, Lewis Kornaherens (age unknown) was standing in waist-deep water near the Elks Club on Folly Island, South Carolina, when a shark grabbed him by both of his legs simultaneously. Lewis hit the shark with his fist, and the animal let go of him. A nearby man then assisted him to shore. The man claimed to have seen about six feet of the attacking shark, but he had been unable to observe the fish more closely because he went to Lewis's aid. Lewis was taken to Roper Hospital in Charleston, where he was treated for lacerated muscles on the left knee and leg. Surgeons used more than 100 stitches to repair his wounds. Lewis was discharged from the hospital on August 28, 1924. After leaving the hospital, Lewis continued to feel pain in his left knee. He was eventually readmitted to the hospital and underwent minor surgery. During the operation, surgeons removed a tooth fragment— which belonged to the attacking shark—from Lewis's kneecap. The hospital sent the tooth fragment to the Charleston Museum, which later sent it to the American Museum of Natural History in New York, where Drs. Eugene Willis Gudger and John Tredwell Nichols positively identified the fragment as a shark's tooth. According to Drs. Gudger and Nichols, it belonged to a species of mackerel shark, presumably a young specimen. Later, Leonard Schultz, a U.S. Navy shark scientist serving with the ISAF and the Smithsonian Institution, examined the tooth fragment and identified it as having come from a lemon shark. (Case #GSAF 1924.07.31)

On June 21, 1933, 15-year-old Dayton Hastie was wading at the mouth of Charleston Harbor on the north end of Morris

Island in South Carolina. While bathing, he noticed what he thought might have been a dorsal fin cutting through the water's rough surface far up the shoreline from his location. Dayton stood up and strained his eyes, attempting to verify what he was seeing. He determined that he must have seen a choppy wave, but he still did not like the idea of swimming in an area where there could be sharks around. Dayton decided to sit down in about three feet of water—a spot where the surf sloped gradually for about six feet and beyond which the slope then merged into a deep drop. Dayton had felt almost certain that by sitting in such shallow water, he was safe from anything large enough to bite. Suddenly, Dayton felt a swirl of water that was instantly followed by an impact. Something had clamped down on his right leg. A tearing pain shot up and down Dayton's leg, and he found himself being pulled outward toward the sea by something that he described as having the power of a horse. Dayton looked down and saw the head of a large shark amid the foam and splashing. The shark had Dayton's leg in its mouth and was shaking it vigorously. Dayton's instincts took over, and he started kicking frantically with his left leg in an attempt to free himself from the shark's grip. Dayton managed to free his right leg only to have the shark bite down on his left one. During the struggle, Dayton had been pulling himself up onto the beach backwards with his hands, while kicking at the shark's rough head. Dayton estimated that the whole ordeal lasted about ten seconds. He was taken to the U.S. Army Hospital at Fort Moultrie, where medical personnel administered first aid. The doctors used more than thirty stitches to close the numerous wounds. Dayton was later transferred to Riverside Infirmary in Charleston, where he remained a patient for two weeks. From this incident, Dayton carried away with him a perfect design of a shark's mouth around his knee. The impression measured ten inches across. Dayton's friend stated that he was standing on the bank at the time of the attack and saw the shark, which was easily eight feet long. During the week before and during the week after the attack, two lemon sharks measuring eight feet in length were taken from the surf within one hundred yards from the site of Dayton's attack. Authorities believe that a lemon shark was involved in this incident. (Case #GSAF 1933.06.21)

Another incident that likely involved a lemon shark occurred in August 1936. Raymond McHenry and James Mitchell-Hedges, both thirteen years old, set out in the shallow waters of Pamlico Sound, off Hatteras Island, in a rowboat to tend the fishing nets they had set the night before. The boys rowed about one hundred to three hundred yards offshore to where the nets were positioned. When they arrived at their destination, the two of them left the rowboat to wade among the nets. The boys were in waist-deep water gathering small fish from the nets when both saw the triangular fin of a large shark cutting through the water toward them. They reached the rowboat and jumped into it just as the shark swished by them. Raymond and James said that the shark swam around the tiny craft, lashing up spray with its tail. It then smashed the bow of the boat and knocked off an oarlock and all the beading around the small vessel. The shark left the scene, but soon after, ten others appeared around the boat. The sharks swam around the boat so closely that the boys said they could have struck them with the oars. One shark suddenly became entangled in one of the fishing nets. The boys quickly loosened the net from its mooring and rowed for shore, towing the enmeshed shark. The other sharks followed the boat to within a few feet from shore. When Raymond and James reached shore, they shot the shark. The animal was eleven feet long and was said to have weighed seven hundred pounds. His jaws measured 4'7" around. Reports described the shark as a sand shark, but people tended to refer to many sharks as "sand sharks" at the time. Years later, a shark biologist examined a photo of the captured shark, and he stated that the shark was most likely a bull or lemon shark.[2]

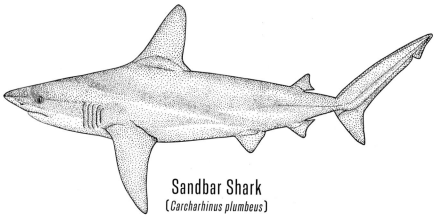

Sandbar Shark
(*Carcharhinus plumbeus*)

Sandbar sharks are compact, stout-bodied sharks that are brownish to gray in color above and bronze to dirty-white below. Their heads are broad with rounded snouts, and the dorsal surface above their gill slits is rather arched in appearance, giving the species a comparatively humped-back profile. Their first dorsal fins are noticeably high and large, triangular, and broad at the base. Their teeth are finely serrated along the edges, triangular, and broad in the upper jaw, whereas the lowers are narrower. The teeth along the outer sections of the jaw are somewhat slanted and have curved margins. They can reach a length of eight feet and weigh in at nearly two hundred pounds. They are one of the more abundant inshore sharks found in the Carolinas, arriving in local waters around May, pupping their young, and hunting inshore waters, estuaries, and saltier water sections of rivers until October. Sandbars could be involved with some attacks in the Carolinas where the attacking species is listed as unknown, and we know of at least two cases where the species is suspect.

On September 9, 1989, thirty-one-year-old Robert Ballard was bitten by what was recorded as a sandbar shark. Robert, a veteran surfer from Virginia Beach, was in the water on a Saturday morning at Salvo on the Outer Banks of North Carolina and was paddling into waves about two hundred yards from shore when a shark, said to have been about three feet long, caught him by surprise. The shark emerged from the water and grabbed him by the right arm, leaving a row of puncture wounds that required 24 stitches to close. Robert then caught a wave and rode it to shore on his belly. Beachgoers placed a towel around his bleeding arm, and from there Robert was treated at two different hospitals. (Case #GSAF 1989.09.09a)

On July 27, 2004, thirteen-year-old Alexis Huesgen was swimming and bodysurfing near the Ocean Boulevard beach access at Carolina Beach, North Carolina, when she was bitten by what records show was likely a six-foot sandbar shark. She had been in the water for about forty-five minutes and was facing the shore when the shark attacked her from behind. It made two strikes—grabbing her arm, shaking it, and then releasing her and swimming away. Swimmers nearby helped her to shore. Alexis sustained serious lacerations to her right forearm, wrist, and fingers. She was taken to New Hanover Regional Medical Center in Wilmington, North Carolina, where surgeons repaired the damage to her arm. (Case #GSAF 2004.07.27b)

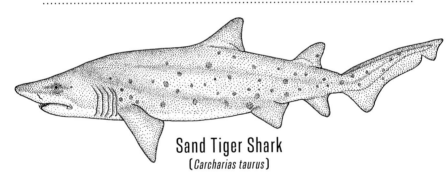

Sand Tiger Shark
(*Carcharias taurus*)

Reaching ten feet in length and stout-bodied—with a pointed snout and a crescent-shaped mouth with long, narrow, daggerlike pointed teeth protruding from it—sand tiger sharks are menacing in appearance. Because of their looks and their proximity to shallow water at times, sand tiger sharks have been blamed for attacks in the Carolinas and in many other parts of the world for which they were most likely not responsible. There was a time when this species was considered as dangerous as the deadly trio, but these days shark experts know them to be rather sluggish and tranquil except when feeding. Not only do these sharks frequent the shallow surf zone, but they also dwell in deep waters—and in North Carolina they are a major attraction at some popular dive sites. Sand tiger sharks, similar to lemon sharks, have two dorsal fins of equal size. They are brownish gray on their dorsal surface and are often marked with yellowish-brown spots on their sides. Their ventral surface is a grayish white in color. They are most abundant in the Carolinas in the warmer months of July through November; however, they are year-round residents in North Carolina. Even though these sharks have been blamed for more attacks than they have committed, they are still considered a potential danger to swimmers and divers. The following cases are reported to have involved a sand tiger shark.

On June 16, 1988, the ISAF reports that a forty-two-year-old diver was bitten by a sand tiger off of Ocracoke, North Carolina. No further details on this incident can be found at this time.

On June 19, 2003, late in the afternoon, thirty-three-year-old Chris White was surfing off the southern part of Masonboro Island, New Hanover County, North Carolina, when he landed right on top of what was reported to have been a sand tiger shark. Chris was testing his nine-foot Bic longboard when he jumped off the back of it to avoid bottoming out as he was coming off of a wave. As he left the board, he landed right on top of the shark. He got off of the animal as quickly as he could, but as he was standing up, the shark grabbed his left hand. Instinctively, Chris jerked his hand away, resulting in lacerations to his knuckles and to his middle finger. The shark also bit through the nail on his ring finger and damaged a nerve between his thumb and index finger. After the attack, the shark swam away, and Chris was taken to a local hospital, where surgeons repaired the nerve damage. (Case #GSAF 2003.06.19)

On August 17, 2011, Trang Aronian and her husband, Matt, were enjoying the ocean near H Avenue Beach Access at Kure Beach, North Carolina. They were about fifteen feet from shore, standing side by side in four to five feet of water, when suddenly Trang felt something strike and tug the top of her foot. The animal immediately let go after its initial strike, and Trang and Matt both witnessed a shark following them to the beach before swimming away. Lifeguards closed the beaches for a short time, and Trang was taken to New Hanover Regional Medical Center in Wilmington, North Carolina, for treatment of lacerations, which required sixty stitches to repair damage she received to the dorsum, sole, and toes of her foot. The couple describes the shark that they saw as five to six feet long. From photographs that he observed, Matt identified what he believes was a sand tiger shark as the species involved. (Case #GSAF 2011.08.17c)

Other cases on file blame a sand shark or sand tiger shark as the attacking species; however, the actual species involved in the incidents is more than likely undetermined. Some people use the generic term *sand shark* to mean any nearshore shark other than a hammerhead, such as a small Atlantic sharpnose, whereas others use the label *sand shark* to refer more specifically to a sand tiger shark.

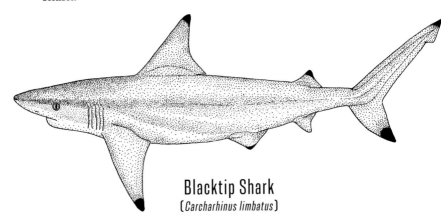

Blacktip Shark
(*Carcharhinus limbatus*)

Blacktip sharks are labeled as one of the most common species involved in shark bite incidents in the Carolinas. Reaching lengths of six feet, these rather stout-bodied sharks sometimes swim in small schools in the Carolinas from May through September, cruising shallow coastal waters in search of small fish, crustaceans, and small cephalopods. They can also be found offshore. These sharks have a somewhat U-shaped snout—not broadly rounded, as with bull sharks and tiger sharks, but tapering to a rounded tip. They have narrow teeth that broaden at their base in the upper jaws and have finely serrated edges along the blade. The lower teeth are slender, also with finely serrated edges. Blacktips range in color from a bronze to a gray dorsal surface with a yellow to white hue on their underside. They have characteristic whitish-gray band markings that extend from the pectorals to the pelvic fins. A distinct black coloration tips each dorsal, second dorsal, and tail fin, but the anal fin is white. The South Carolina state-record blacktip weighed 133 pounds. Attacks by blacktips in the Carolinas include the following encounters:

On July 14, 1997, fifty-year-old Flint Cowden was swimming at night near 60th Avenue North in Myrtle Beach, South Carolina, in chest-deep water about fifty yards from shore when he felt something clamp down on his left leg. Flint described the sensation as feeling as though he had stepped into a bear trap. Flint received a 7" × 8" bite to his left calf. Investigators thought that the species involved was a blacktip shark. (Case #GSAF 1997.07.14)

On June 14, 2012, four people suffered minor injuries by sharks within a ten- to fifteen-minute period within an eight-mile stretch of shallow to chest-deep water from 72nd Avenue to 82nd Avenue at Myrtle Beach, South Carolina. All victims were bitten on their feet, calves, or both. One victim also received a bite to the hand. That day, the water surface temperature was 78.1 degrees Fahrenheit, and the ocean was "murkier than usual," according to lifeguard Denny Starr. The minor injuries that each victim suffered—in such a short span of time and in close proximity to each other—suggest that a school of blacktip sharks was likely swimming along the surf zone shoreline. (Cases #GSAF 2012.06.14a/b/c/d)

There are many other cases of shark bites resulting in minor injuries in the Carolinas that are listed as unidentified. Many of these bites likely originated from blacktips.

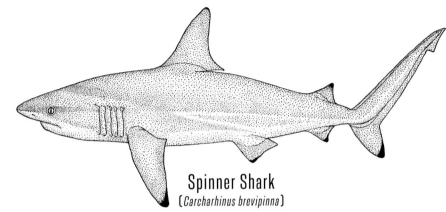

Spinner Shark
(*Carcharhinus brevipinna*)

Spinner sharks are most commonly found in the Carolinas from July through October. Adult spinner sharks resemble blacktips in that each of their fins—dorsal, second dorsal, pectoral, and lower caudal—are tipped in black. A spinner shark also has the dark marking on its anal fin, whereas the blacktip's anal fin is white with no markings. Spinners are more slender than blacktips, and their snout is more of a V-shape than the U-shaped snout of blacktips. Their teeth are broad-based in the upper and lower jaw, tapering to a more slender crown. The upper teeth are finely serrated along the edges of the crown, but the lower teeth are smooth-edged. These sharks are known to leap out of the water, spinning when in pursuit of prey. They are also prized gamefish for anglers because of this leaping and spinning behavior when hooked. Because blacktips also tend to display this jumping, spinning behavior, people often confuse the two species. Spinners can grow to a length of six to possibly eight feet and can weigh in at as much as 123 pounds.

No attacks in the Carolinas conclusively identify a spinner shark as an attacking species; however, many of the cases where the species is officially undetermined could, in fact, be spinner shark bites.

Concluding Remarks

I hope I have shown the extreme rarity of shark attacks on humans throughout the world by examining these occurrences in North and South Carolina waters. In the United States, the Carolinas rank in the top five of the most likely places to encounter a shark, which makes this region the perfect area for shark attack research. Yet, out of the millions of water users from 1817 to 2019, which spans 203 years, only 242 cases of confirmed shark attacks have been documented for the Carolinas. Out of this small number, twenty-five recorded deaths resulted from shark attacks, and out of that number, thirteen of those deaths occurred out at sea and involved shipwreck victims. By placing these numbers into perspective with the date ranges of the study, I have shown that the chance of encountering a shark off of the Carolina Coasts is slim to nonexistent.

Sharks are a valuable part of our oceans' natural world. They are fascinating creatures that are vulnerable to endangerment and extinction without our proper care and monitoring. They deserve great respect for their capabilities of the harm they can inflict, but they do not deserve the senseless slaughter they have endured over the years by our human hands.

If I have provided practical solutions for how to avoid encountering a shark, and if I can help reduce the amount of fear in the eyes of the general public concerning these fish—instead replacing such fear with the healthy respect they deserve—while instilling a sense of value and worth for sharks in the minds of my readers, then I have accomplished a small contribution toward the survivability of these animals. This is my hope for this book.

7 Studying Shark Attacks

The Shark Research Institute, the Global Shark Attack File, and the International Shark Attack File are three of the most dependable and referenced sources regarding shark attacks and shark study statistics on which marine biologists, researchers, investigators, medical professionals, scientists, reporters, authors, and those interested in sharks rely.

The Shark Research Institute

In 1991, the Shark Research Institute (SRI), which is the oldest shark conservation research organization in the United States, was formed at Princeton University. The idea for this 501(c)(3) non-profit organization came about from university faculty, local divers, and members of the international multidisciplinary Explorers Club, each with a great desire to sponsor and conduct research on all shark species and their natural habitat, which would aid in the protection of these animals and would promote a positive message on the true value that they are to the global ecosystem. Today, SRI engages a vast network of marine biologists, shark behaviorists, and others who represent not only various branches of science but also other disciplines—including genetics, medicine, physics, computer science, education, law, history, and filmmaking. This diversity of perspectives within the organization is a source of unique and valuable strength in the overall study of sharks around the world. SRI currently operates various field offices internationally, including permanent stations in the United States and Canada and seasonal locations in the Caribbean, Costa Rica, East Africa, India, the Philippines, and throughout the Pacific. Ongoing research from SRI members includes visual and satellite tracking, behavioral and DNA studies, environmental advocacy, publications, and public education on sharks. SRI's research efforts and techniques help protect sharks and enable scientists to determine locations in the world that need a greater focus on conservation efforts.

In hopes of changing the general perception of fear and misunderstanding toward sharks, SRI also offers opportunities for the public to see sharks for themselves through sponsored diving expeditions. For example, in 2017 SRI's sponsored dives included two trips to Afuera, along the Yucatan Peninsula of Mexico, which is home to the largest massing of whale sharks in the world. SRI also offered fossil shark tooth hunts at different locations throughout that summer and sponsored shark tagging trips in the fall. SRI also notifies their followers of other expeditions from affiliated organizations.

SRI is passionately involved with teaching the public about sharks, again with the goal of eliminating false fears and misunderstandings about them, through outreach educational programs. SRI team members can regularly be found leading presentations on sharks at schools, museums, marinas, surf competitions, aquariums, libraries, dive expositions, and other public events. Members also consistently reach out to legislators and other government officials regarding laws and regulations that affect sharks and their environment to ensure that elected officials at all levels are proactively working to maintain proper protections for sharks. As of this writing, at least thirteen American states (not including North and South Carolina)—as well as Chile, Guam, Honduras, the Marshall Islands, the Commonwealth of the Northern Mariana Islands, and Taiwan—have now passed laws banning the shark fin trade, thus helping to reduce the massive, senseless slaughter of these animals simply for their fins. This is just one example of the many success stories in which SRI has played a part.[1] Visit www.sharks.org to learn more.

Marie Levine, PhD, is the founder and current executive director of SRI. Under her stewardship, the organization has expanded its membership to more than seventeen thousand people, all of whom are working with research and conservation projects in Canada, Costa Rica, Ecuador, Honduras, India, Mexico, Mozambique, the Philippines, Seychelles, South Africa, Tanzania, the United Kingdom, and the United States. In addition to articles in scientific journals and chapters in shark information books, Marie Levine has authored children's books about sharks and has edited popular books on sharks for adults. During her stint as the senior liaison officer of the Natal Sharks Board in KwaZulu-Natal, South Africa (now known as the KwaZulu-Natal Sharks Board Maritime Centre of Excellence), Dr. Levine reestablished the South African Shark Attack File. She has also worked and dived with sharks in forty-three countries. As a Fellow of the Explorers Club, she has led five Flag Expeditions and in 2001 was inducted into the Women Divers Hall of Fame and subsequently served on its Board of Directors.

The Global Shark Attack File

In 1993 SRI took over the responsibility of maintaining the Global Shark Attack File (GSAF), one of the largest shark–human encounter data banks containing the most accurate, up-to-date information regarding shark–human incidents dating back as far as ca. 725 B.C. (B.C.E.) up to the present day.

In 1990 a group of physicians, surgeons, and medical examiners created the file strictly for medical professionals who were interested in gathering data on shark attacks and making the information universally accessible to those seeking information on shark bite treatment protocols. When SRI took over, the file became accessible not only to medical professionals but also to marine biologists, shark behaviorists, law enforcement officials, those in the conservation community, the media, and even the public seeking accurate information on shark–human encounters. Sensitive information such as wound photos and medical records are not available to the public; however, readers can access detailed information on each case through the website, www.sharkattackfile.net.

The GSAF functions using data compiled from various on-site and off-site sources that include shark researchers, medical professionals, law enforcement officials, EMS personnel, lifeguards, and shark research institute investigators in similar positions to mine. GSAF's goal is to provide the most accurate information on shark–human encounters through forensic examination of both historical and current cases. GSAF experts conduct these detailed investigations to help establish patterns of shark behavior and human activities that may have triggered a shark-related incident. For the protection of sharks and the safety of humans using our oceans, the GSAF hopes to show the actual *infrequency* of shark attacks, thus eliminating the exaggerated fear that many people possess of these animals and instead replacing that fear with a desire for conservation of all shark species. But the GSAF *is* interested in actual shark attack numbers and will document cases that potentially involve shark attacks that many other organizations may discard. I discuss these types of cases earlier in this book. GSAF researchers have also debunked cases that other groups have labeled as "shark attacks" when clear evidence presented through detailed analysis seems to prove otherwise.

The current director of the GSAF is Ralph S. Collier. Collier is internationally recognized as the leading authority on Pacific Coast shark attacks. He is also the president and founder of the Shark Research Committee. Having studied shark–human interactions for more than fifty years and being published in many scientific journals and research symposium volumes, Collier is a reliable and favored expert for the media regarding shark attack information. He has interviewed more white shark attack survivors, witnesses, and rescuers than has any other shark researcher, and his work has been cited in hundreds of newspapers, magazines, and television reports as well as in more than three dozen documentary films. Collier pioneered the technique for using the distance between tooth impressions to determine shark species and size, and he was the first researcher to cite the significance of recurring locations concerning white shark attacks. He is the author of *Shark Attacks of the Twentieth Century: From the Pacific Coast of North America,* a landmark book on great white shark attacks.

The International Shark Attack File

The International Shark Attack File (ISAF) is probably the most popular and well-known global database of shark attack incidents on humans. The file originated from funding provided by the Office of Naval Research in an attempt to collect and study cases of shark attacks on servicemen during World War II. The file was funded for ten years, from 1958 to 1968. During that period shark experts established the ISAF's standard system for collecting and studying shark attack incidents from around the world. After 1968 the file was relocated and temporarily housed at the Mote Marine Laboratory in Sarasota, Florida. Since 1988 the Florida Museum of Natural History, located on the University of Florida campus, has permanently housed the file. The ISAF remains under the direction of the American Elasmobranch Society (AES)—a panel of professional scientists dedicated to the study of cartilaginous fishes (sharks, skates, and rays).

The current director of the ISAF is Gavin Naylor, who was formerly with the Medical University of South Carolina and the College of Charleston. Naylor has been studying sharks, skates, and rays for nearly thirty years. The former director, George H. Burgess, retired in 2017. Burgess has worked with the University of Florida for more than 40 years and remains one of the most consulted sources for the media concerning shark attack incidents.

The GSAF Shark Bite Investigation Method

The GSAF has qualified investigators stationed throughout the world actively investigating shark attacks. The information collected from these thorough shark attack investigations helps GSAF and other researchers determine common or reoccurring events in a specific geographical area where a shark attack occurred. When shark researchers collect information from these investigations over many years, common factors begin to emerge—and they give us a glimpse into local shark population habits and shark species behavior as well as into any human activities that are associated with shark attack incidents. When multiple cases in an area are added to the GSAF's continually growing shark attack databank, worldwide patterns of shark behavior and shark–human interactions begin to take shape. Individual shark attack investigations as a whole are the pieces of a broader worldwide puzzle of shark attack incidents that, when put together, become a valuable tool that aids researchers, lifesavers, educators, and investigators to better understand the actual threat that sharks pose to humans in various situations and locations. The GSAF also uses the data to help those involved in shark attack research learn ways to best inform the public about how to lessen their chances of placing themselves in a potential shark attack situation.

A thorough shark attack investigation begins as soon as GSAF staff learns of a shark bite incident in a particular area. Local authorities usually send an alert to the investigator who is covering the region where the bite occurred—or, at times, an investigator knows of a shark bite in their geographic area even before other GSAF members and will begin the investigation immediately while also informing GSAF headquarters.

As soon as possible after a shark bite has occurred, a GSAF investigator contacts the victim or the victim's family to (a) request copies of medical records pertaining to the shark bite and (b) conduct an interview to gather detailed information that only the victim or the victim's family can answer. After getting basic information— such as the victim's name, birthdate, height, weight, contact information, time, date, and attack's specific location—the GSAF investigator collects other pertinent information about the victim. This includes a detailed description of all clothing and jewelry that the victim was wearing, a description of any injuries that the victim may have suffered prior to the attack, and whether the victim was menstruating at the time of the attack. The GSAF investigator also asks the victim or family what activity the victim was engaged in prior to receiving the shark bite. If the victim was using a boogie board, float, surfboard, or other object, the GSAF investigator records details such as length, make, and color of the object. All of this information helps investigators and researchers determine factors about the victim that possibly attracted the shark's attention.

The GSAF also records any important environmental factors that could have been inviting to a shark—including any fish, bird, or dolphin activity observed prior to the attack; the victim's distance from jetties, fishing piers, river mouths, channels, or other features; any fishing activity at the attack location; and the depth of the water in which the victim had been swimming, surfing, boogie boarding, or other activity during or prior to the attack. Various factors help the investigator gain insight into the attack location and attack sequence: the direction of the current; sea temperature; sea description (calm, choppy, swells, etc.); weather details (sunny, cloudy, rainy, air temperature, etc.); what direction (shoreward or seaward) the victim was facing prior to the bite; the number of people in the water around the victim; and an approximate number of people on the beach.

If the victim was a diver, the GSAF gathers detailed information about the diving suit—including the color of the suit, mask, and fins. The victim or family is asked if the victim was using Self-Contained Underwater Breathing Apparatus (SCUBA) equipment and if the victim was spearfishing at the time of the attack. If spearfishing *was* involved, then the GSAF records another series of details, including the number of fish shot prior to the attack and what species these were, where the anglers were placing the fish during the moment that the attack occurred (e.g., on a stringer, on a float, or on a boat), the distance the victim was from the dive boat when they were attacked, the water's depth where the attack took place, the victim's location in the water at the time of the attack (surface, ascending, descending, or on the bottom, and if submerged, at what depth the attack occurred). If the victim was attacked while diving from a boat, then the GSAF records information such as boat type, hull color, and boat length.

The GSAF investigator also contacts others involved with the shark attack for any additional information that they may be able to provide from the scene or regarding the shark bite injury. These people include witnesses, medics, rescuers, police and fire officials, lifeguards, and medical personnel.

The GSAF questions the victim or family members about the shark involved in the attack. If someone saw the shark prior to, during, or after the attack, then the GSAF first asks the witness if they can identify the species they saw. If they are unsure, then the GSAF asks for details about the animal—such as the number of sharks witnessed, an estimate of the animal's length and mass, a description of its eyes, and the shape of the snout and tail. These details, if answered, can aid researchers in proper species identification.

Investigators also examine the attack sequence. The answers to these questions can aid researchers in determining possible species involvement as well as potential motivations for the attack. The investigator asks victims, family, and witnesses to describe the duration or time frame of not only the initial strike but also of the entire attack. Also included are questions involving how many actual strikes the victim suffered; if the shark pushed, pulled, or submerged the victim; if the victim attempted to strike back; and, if so, the shark's reaction. The investigator also makes inquiries regarding any rescue efforts that others may have attempted—and, if so, the effect that it had on the outcome of the attack. It helps to know whether the shark injured any rescuers—and, if so, what injuries the rescuers sustained. The GSAF also explores the shark's behavior prior to, during, and after the attack. Last, the investigator inquires about whether the shark attack seemed deliberate, frenzied, or accidental, in their opinion.

A critical element with any shark bite investigation is to collect clear photos of the victim's wounds prior to surgery or any bandaging. Either medical personnel or GSAF employees perform this task—usually in an operating or surgical preparation room. Ideal photos include specific measurements of the body part bitten, the circumference and width of the shark bite, and the distance between each tooth impression. Each of these features—along with observing the shape and other characteristics of the wound—aid in determining the sequence of the attack as well as the size and species of shark involved in an incident. With or without photos, however, GSAF always asks interviewees for a detailed description of the victim's wounds.

Interviewees are also asked if anyone recovered any tooth fragments from a wound. Although rare, if tooth fragments are found and can be studied, then shark bite experts can usually make a positive identification of the attacking species.

The investigator also records information on any first aid and treatment procedures that people may have administered at the attack site as well as details regarding who treated the victim, where the victim was treated at each interval after the attack, any effects of such treatments, and contact information for anyone involved.

After gathering as many details as possible on a shark bite case, investigators then compile all the data and record it on a standardized form in order to make it easier for scientists to identify general factors and shark behavioral patterns as follows:

— Place and date of the incident, longitude and latitude, and distance to reference points (e.g., places).

— Name and body description of the victim (including clothes and jewelry) and any equipment used by the victim, including harpoons and surfboards.

— General data on weather, water, and environmental factors at the time of the incident. Also noted is the distance to the shore, the time of the attack, the water depth, and the victim's position. GSAF supplements this information by providing sketches of the scene that depict details about the shore, canals, and rock formations in that immediate area.

— Narrative version of the event sequence, also including the victim's subjective impressions and reports from witnesses.

— Medical description of the wounds by the doctor who treated the victim either in the trauma center or in the operating room. Investigators also describe any damage to surfboards or other objects that have been chewed up, and they add sketches on the location and extent of the victim's wounds as well as close-up photographs of the bite and wounds.

— Description of first aid measures taken and medical care, including any administered antibiotics.

— Description of the sequence of events surrounding the accident investigation. Discussion and analysis of these data, sketches, or bite damage serve as reference for special descriptions.

Conclusions.[2]

Reporting an Incident to the Global Shark Attack File

Although the GSAF has active investigators stationed in various places throughout the world, some areas still are not always accessible to field support staff. To compensate for this, the GSAF encourages members and website visitors to participate in its ongoing shark–human interaction research. If you would like to report a shark attack incident or have information on historical shark–human cases that you would like to submit to the GSAF, you can use one of the following methods with resources available at www.sharkattackfile.net:

— Email the GSAF at report@sharkattackfile.net.

~ Contact the regional GSAF investigator who is stationed in the geographic area where the incident occurred by clicking on the "GSAF Investigators" tab.

~ Download the detailed GSAF questionnaire for male or female (for males: http://sharkattackfile.net/Questionnaire_male.pdf; for females: http://sharkattackfile.net/Questionnaire_female .pdf), complete the form, and mail it to Global Shark Attack File, Shark Research Institute, P.O. Box 40, Princeton, NJ 08542, USA, or email it to the curator Marie Levine at marie@sharks .org.

~ Complete and submit the "short form" found within the "Report an Incident" tab or at http://www.sharkattackfile.net /reportform6.

Carolina Shark Attack Incidents

1817–2019

The following list stops at the end of 2019; however, by nature it is a continuing work in progress. It is a compilation of all shark attacks that investigators have recorded as occurring in North and South Carolina waters from 1817 to the present time, including shark–human encounters and even incidents that are likely shark related but remain unconfirmed. The list is continually expanded as new cases occur or are discovered; it is the most up-to-date and accurate record on the subject likely found anywhere. For purposes of this book, I have reduced the list to display *Date, Outcome, Area,* and *Location* only. For more detailed information on each case, click on the "Incident Log" tab from the home page of the GSAF website: www .sharkattackfile.net. From there you can locate each incident listed below by date and click on the case file number to access additional information, including the time of day in which the incident occurred, what the victim was doing prior to the attack, the attacking species (if known), the injury or injuries that the victim sustained, any potential environmental causative factors contributing to the incident, sources, and other data as available.

Outcome Abbreviations

F = fatal (human killed by a shark)

NF = nonfatal (human survived shark attack)

PB = postmortem bites (shark bites to human occurred after death)

Pro = Provoked incident.

QI = questionable incident (shark attack or encounter is in question)

SAPTDU = shark attack prior to death not ruled out or confirmed

SE = shark encounter (shark–human encounter not resulting in a shark bite to human)

SI = serious injury (human survived shark attack but sustained serious injuries)
SINC = shark involvement not confirmed (shark as attacking species is most likely
but is not confirmed)

Note: Several incidents listed with the same date (*) correspond to
events involving multiple cases. "Ca." refers to "circa.", meaning the
specific date is not accurately known. A '+' symbol indicates that
more than one type of attack occurred within one outcome.

DATE	OUTCOME	AREA	LOCATION
June 24, 1817	F	SC	Charleston Harbor in Charleston County
Ca. 1837	SAPTDU	SC	Southern Wharf
Summer 1837	NF	SC	Magwoods Wharf, Charleston Harbor, Charleston County
Ca. 1840	F	SC	Charleston Harbor in Charleston County
Summer 1847	SAPTDU	SC	Between Castle Pinckney and Wharf
Ca. 1847	NF (SI)	SC	Unknown
1852	F	SC	Mount Pleasant in Charleston County
July 13, 1853	F (QI)	SC	Charleston Harbor in Charleston County
Sept. or Oct. 1853	NF (QI)	NC	Off the coast of Morehead City at *The Atlanta,* a ship that sank just inside the bar
1853 or 1854	SAPTDU	SC	Off the Battery (Downtown Charleston landmark)
Sept. 30, 1855	NF	NC	Cape Hatteras
Sept. 1863	SE	SC	Stono Inlet near Charleston
July 27, 1870	NF (SI)	NC	Southport
Sept. 8, 1881	SAPTDU	NC	Elizabeth City in Pasquotank County
Ca. 1883 or near it	SE	SC	Near Castle Pinckney in Charleston
1883	F	SC	Unknown
1883	SAPTDU	SC	Bulls Bay near Charleston
Sept. 28, 1883	NF (QI)	NC	Off the coast of Morehead City at *The Atlanta,* a ship that sank just inside the bar
1888	SE	NC	Wrightsville Beach in New Hanover County

DATE	OUTCOME	AREA	LOCATION
Sept. 15, 1894	NF	NC	New Bern in Craven County
Sept. 1895	SE	NC	Off the coast of Southport, near mouth of Cape Fear River, near Fort Caswell in Brunswick County
June 21, 1896	NF	SC	Charleston
Sept. 6, 1897	NF	SC	Elliott Cut, Charleston County
1898	NF	SC	Ramshorn Creek, Cooper River, Beaufort County
Aug. 21, 1900	NF (SI)	NC	Southport
1900 to 1905	F	NC	Ocracoke Inlet
1905	SE	NC	Cape Lookout
July 1905	F	NC	Ocracoke Inlet
July 29, 1905	F	NC	Davis Shore, in the waters of the Core Sound, east of Beaufort
July 1907	NF	SC	Small creek near Coles Island
Oct. 26, 1911	F	SC	Off the coast of Charleston
July 23, 1912	NF (SI)	SC	Sullivan's Island
July 12, 1912 or 13	F (QI)	SC	Off the coast of Charleston
Jan. 14, 1915	SE	NC	Somewhere off the coast of North Carolina
July 27, 1916	NF (SI)	NC	New Bern, near Atlantic City in Craven County
Prior to July 17, 1916	NF (SI; QI)	NC	Somewhere between Hatteras Island and Beaufort
June 3, 1917	NF	SC	Calibogue Sound
May 29, 1919	NF	SC	James Island Sound
July 31, 1924	NF	SC	Folly Island, near Charleston
Aug. 2, 1925	NF	SC	Folly Island, near Charleston
Aug. 5, 1929	NF	SC	Fort Moultrie
June 16, 1933	NF	SC	Folly Island, near Charleston
June 21, 1933	NF	SC	North end of Morris Island at the mouth of Charleston Harbor
July 16, 1933	NF (QI)	SC	Charleston

DATE	OUTCOME	AREA	LOCATION
Aug. 28, 1933	NF	SC	Pawley's Island, near Charleston
Sept. 21, 1935	F	NC	Brown's Inlet on the New River in Onslow County
Aug. 1936	SE	NC	Frisco, in Pamlico Sound off Hatteras Island
Nov. 13, 1937*	F	NC	Off the coast of Cape Hatteras
Nov. 13, 1937*	F	NC	Off the coast of Cape Hatteras
Nov. 13, 1937*	F	NC	Off the coast of Cape Hatteras
1938	SE	NC	One of the sounds near Wilmington, in New Hanover County, near the boat landing of Mrs. W. S. Willard
July 18, 1938	NF	SC	Charleston
June 30, 1940	NF (SI)	NC	Holden Beach in Brunswick County
July 13, 1940*	NF	SC	Folly Beach
July 13, 1940*	NF	SC	Folly Beach
Aug. 1, 1941	NF	SC	Sullivan's Island, at the entrance to Charleston Harbor
Dec. 4, 1943*	NF	SC	Off the coast of Charleston
Dec. 4, 1943*	F	SC	Off the coast of Charleston
Dec. 4, 1943*	F	SC	Off the coast of Charleston
Dec. 4, 1943*	F	SC	Off the coast of Charleston
Dec. 4, 1943*	F	SC	Off the coast of Charleston
Dec. 4, 1943*	F	SC	Off the coast of Charleston
Dec. 4, 1943*	F	SC	Off the coast of Charleston
Dec. 4, 1943*	F	SC	Off the coast of Charleston
Dec. 4, 1943*	F	SC	Off the coast of Charleston
Dec. 4, 1943*	F	SC	Off the coast of Charleston
Dec. 4, 1943*	F	SC	Off the coast of Charleston
May 8, 1945	F	NC	Ocracoke Inlet
July 25, 1949	NF	SC	Okatee River in Jasper County
Oct. 5, 1951	PB	SC	400 miles off the coast of South Carolina waters

DATE	OUTCOME	AREA	LOCATION
July 27, 1952	NF (Pro)	SC	Seabrook Beach
Sept. 21, 1953	SE	SC	Charleston
Aug. 4, 1955	NF (Pro)	SC	Windy Hill, near Myrtle Beach, in Horry County
July 25, 1956	NF	SC	Isle of Palms in Charleston County
July 15, 1957	F	NC	Salter Path on Atlantic Beach in Carteret County
Aug. 14, 1959	NF (Pro)	SC	Charleston
Sept. 26, 1959	SE	SC	Near the Marine Corps Air Station Beaufort boat docks on Albergotti Creek, Beaufort County
June 29, 1960	NF (Pro)	SC	Little River Beach in Horry County
Aug. 1960	F (QI)	SC	Marine Corps Recruit Depot Parris Island
Sept. 24, 1960	NF (Pro)	SC	Atlantic Beach in Horry County
Aug. 16, 1961	NF (SI)	SC	Pawleys Island in Georgetown County
June 10, 1962	NF	SC	Hilton Head Island in Beaufort County
July 28, 1962	NF	SC	Hilton Head Island in Beaufort County
July 1967	QI	SC	Unknown
June 16, 1968, or July 16, 1968	NF	SC	Stono Inlet, near Charleston, in Charleston County
Sept. 1970	NF	SC	Unknown
Sept. 25, 1971	NF	NC	Emerald Isle in Carteret County
June 23, 1975	NF	SC	North Myrtle Beach in Horry County
June 23, 1975	NF	SC	Windy Hill, near Myrtle Beach in Horry County
1976	QI	NC	Yaupon Beach in Brunswick County, in front of the condos
Aug. 26, 1976	NF	NC	Emerald Isle, near the pier in Morehead City, Carteret County
July 27, 1978	SE + PB	SC	In the Atlantic Ocean off the coast of Charleston
Late July 1980	SE	NC	Emerald Isle, near the Emerald Isle Pier in Carteret County

DATE	OUTCOME	AREA	LOCATION
Aug. 11, 1980	NF	NC	Ocean Isle in Brunswick County
May 1982	SAPTDU	SC	Daws Island in the Broad River, near Beaufort
June 26, 1982	NF	SC	Isle of Palms in Charleston County
Nov. 1982	NF	SC	Isle of Palms in Charleston County
Jan. 24, 1983	NF (Pro)	NC	60 miles southeast of Beaufort
1983	NF (Pro)	NC	North Carolina coast
1984	NF	SC	Unknown
1984	NF	SC	Unknown
1985	NF	SC	Unknown
1985	NF	SC	Unknown
1985	NF	SC	Unknown
1985	NF	SC	Unknown
July 19, 1985	NF (SI)	SC	Folly Beach in Charleston County
Aug. 22, 1985	NF	SC	Palmetto Dunes Oceanfront Resort on Hilton Head Island in Beaufort County
Dec. 10, 1985	NF	NC	New Hanover County
July 9, 1986	NF	SC	Myrtle Beach in Horry County
Aug. 19, 1986	NF	NC	Masonboro Inlet in New Hanover County
May 25, 1987	NF	SC	Myrtle Beach in Horry County
July 11, 1987	SE	SC	Winyah Bay between Charleston and Myrtle Beach
1988	NF	SC	Unknown
June 9, 1988	NF (SI)	SC	In front of the Sea Pines Beach Club on Hilton Head Island in Beaufort County
June 16, 1988	NF	NC	Ocracoke in Hyde County
Sept. 9, 1989	NF	NC	Salvo in Dare County
Oct. 8, 1989	SAPTDU	NC	Between Wrightsville Beach and Carolina Beach in New Hanover County
Aug. 3, 1990	QI	NC	Snow's Cut Channel on the Intracoastal Waterway in New Hanover County

DATE	OUTCOME	AREA	LOCATION
Aug. 1, 1991	SAPTDU	NC	Southeast of New Topsail Inlet in Pender County
Aug. 2, 1991	NF	SC	Unknown
Aug. 26, 1991	NF	SC	Myrtle Beach in Horry County
May 31, 1992	SAPTDU	NC	The wreck of the *U-352* (located 26 miles south of Morehead City)
June 1993	SE	NC	Olde Point Creek or Nixon Creek, Hampstead, in Pender County
Aug. 15, 1993	NF (SI)	NC	Pamlico Sound
Sept. 26, 1994	NF	SC	North Forest Beach, near Hilton Head Island in Beaufort County
June 17, 1995	NF	SC	Garden City Beach in Horry County
Early July 1995	NF (Pro)	SC	Myrtle Beach, off 29th Ave. in Horry County
July 24, 1995	NF	SC	Pawleys Island in Georgetown County
July 28, 1995	NF	SC	Pawleys Island in Georgetown County
Aug. 10, 1995	NF	SC	Ocean Lakes Campground, south of Myrtle Beach in Horry County
Aug 13, 1995	PB	NC	Emerald Isle in Carteret County
Aug. 21, 1995	SE	NC	Cape Lookout Bight
Aug. 22, 1995	NF	NC	Wrightsville Beach in New Hanover County
Aug. 25, 1995	NF	NC	Off Masonboro Island in New Hanover County
Aug. 31, 1995	NF	SC	Myrtle Beach in Horry County
Sept. 3, 1995	NF	NC	Bald Head Island in Brunswick County
1995	NF	SC	Pawleys Island in Georgetown County
1996	NF	NC	Unknown
June 25, 1996	NF	SC	Fripp Island in Beaufort County
Sept. 1, 1996	NF (SINC)	SC	Garden City Beach in Horry County
June 14, 1997	NF (QI)	SC	Unknown
July 14, 1997	NF	SC	Myrtle Beach in Horry County
July 17, 1997	NF	SC	Myrtle Beach in Horry County

DATE	OUTCOME	AREA	LOCATION
Feb. 26, 1999	SE	NC	Frying Pan Shoals, 18 miles southeast of Cape Fear
July 6, 1999	NF	SC	Charleston
Aug. 16, 1999	NF	SC	Grand Strand at Myrtle Beach in Horry County
Aug. 24, 1999	NF	NC	Fort Fisher in New Hanover County
Sept. 10, 1999	NF	SC	Isle of Palms in Charleston County
July 6, 2000	NF	NC	Pine Island at Corolla in Currituck County
July 16, 2000	NF	NC	Holden Beach in Brunswick County
July 17, 2000	NF	NC	Oceanic Pier at Wrightsville Beach in New Hanover County
Aug. 11, 2000	NF (SINC)	NC	Emerald Isle in Carteret County
Aug. 21, 2000	NF (SI; SINC)	NC	Bogue Banks, Emerald Isle, in Carteret County
Sept. 16, 2000	NF	SC	Isle of Palms in Charleston County
Oct. 2, 2000	NF	NC	Wrightsville Beach in New Hanover County
May 20, 2001	NF	SC	Fripp Island in Beaufort County
May 21, 2001	NF	SC	Coligny Beach at Hilton Head Island in Beaufort County
June 3, 2001	NF	SC	Isle of Palms, off 21st Ave. in Charleston County
July 3, 2001	NF (QI)	SC	Isle of Palms in Charleston County
July 26, 2001	NF	SC	Near 23rd Ave., Myrtle Beach, Horry County
Aug. 5, 2001	NF	SC	Near 70th Ave., Myrtle Beach, Horry County
Sept. 3, 2001*	F	NC	Avon, Hatteras Island, Outer Banks, in Dare County
Sept. 3, 2001*	NF (SI)	NC	Avon, Hatteras Island, Outer Banks in Dare County
Sept. 7, 2001	NF (SINC)	SC	Waites Island in Horry County
Sept. 15, 2001	NF	NC	North Topsail Beach in Onslow County

DATE	OUTCOME	AREA	LOCATION
May 4, 2002	NF	SC	Litchfield Beach in Georgetown
July 4, 2002	NF	NC	Wrightsville Beach in New Hanover County
July 20, 2002	NF	NC	Emerald Isle in Carteret County
July 26, 2002	NF	SC	Myrtle Beach in Horry County
Aug. 5, 2002	NF	NC	Topsail Beach in Pender County
June 15, 2003	NF (SINC)	SC	Pawleys Island in Georgetown County
June 19, 2003	NF	NC	Wrightsville Beach on Masonboro Island in New Hanover County
Sept. 13, 2003	NF (Pro)	SC	Isle of Palms
2003	NF (QI)	SC	Unknown
July 27, 2004	NF	NC	Carolina Beach in New Hanover County
July 28, 2004	NF	NC	Rodanthe in Dare County
Sept. 4, 2004	NF	SC	Myrtle Beach, north of Apache Pier in Horry County
May 2, 2005	SE	SC/NC	Between Charleston and Southport
June 7, 2005	NF	SC	Kiawah Island in Charleston County
July 15, 2005	NF	NC	Holden Beach in Brunswick County
Aug. 6, 2005	NF	SC	Isle of Palms in Charleston County
Aug. 12, 2005	NF	NC	Carolina Beach, in front of Texas Ave., New Hanover County
Aug. 21, 2005	NF	SC	Myrtle Beach, near 34th Avenue in Horry County
Aug. 22, 2005	NF	SC	North Myrtle Beach, near 6th Avenue South in Horry County
Sept. 5, 2005	NF (SI)	NC	North Topsail Beach in Onslow County at the mouth of the New River Inlet
Sept. 11, 2005	SAPTDU	SC	Folly Beach in Charleston County
Sept. 20, 2005	NF	SC	North Myrtle Beach, 48th Avenue South, behind Beach Cove, in Horry County
June 7, 2006	NF	SC	Coligny Beach at Hilton Head Island in Beaufort County

DATE	OUTCOME	AREA	LOCATION
June 8, 2006	NF	SC	DeBordieu Beach in Georgetown County, near Pawleys Island
July 12, 2006	NF	SC	Kiawah Island in Charleston County
July 17, 2006	NF	SC	Singleton Beach on Hilton Head Island in Beaufort County
Aug. 2006	NF	NC	Masonboro Inlet in New Hanover County
Sept. 16, 2006	NF	NC	Onslow Beach in Onslow County
May 26, 2007	NF	SC	Garden City Beach in Horry County
July 17, 2007	NF	NC	Eastern part of Atlantic Beach in front of the Tar Landing Villas, Carteret County
July 18, 2007	NF	NC	North Topsail Beach in Onslow County
Aug. 9, 2007	NF	SC	Isle of Palms County Park in Charleston County
Aug. 9, 2007	NF (SI)	SC	Isle of Palms in Charleston County, off Beachwood East in the Wild Dunes Resort area
Aug. 19, 2007	NF	SC	Between Myrtle Beach and Surfside Beach, to the south at Lakewood Campground
Aug. 22, 2007	NF (Pro)	NC	Fort Fisher Aquarium in Fort Fisher, New Hanover County
Sept. 4, 2007	NF	SC	Sullivan's Island/Charleston County/ at Station 23
May 26, 2008	NF (SI; SINC)	NC	"In front of campsite #3," Hammocks Beach State Park, Bear Island, Onslow County
June 1, 2008	NF	SC	Cherry Grove in Horry County
June 26, 2008	NF	SC	Isle of Palms in Charleston County
July 5, 2008	NF	SC	North Litchfield Beach in Georgetown County
July 10, 2008	NF	NC	Emerald Isle in Carteret County
July 11, 2008	NF	SC	Isle of Palms in Charleston County
July 13, 2008	SE (SINC)	NC	Carolina Beach in New Hanover County

DATE	OUTCOME	AREA	LOCATION
July 24, 2008	NF	NC	Surf City, Topsail Island, Pender County
July 24, 2008	NF	NC	Surf City, Topsail Island, Pender County
Aug. 18, 2008	NF (SINC)	SC	16th Avenue South, North Myrtle Beach, Horry County
Aug. 22, 2008	NF	NC	In front of the Surf Condos, Surf City, Topsail Island, Pender County
July 22, 2009	NF	NC	Holden Beach in Brunswick County
Sept. 12, 2009	SAPTDU	NC	Off mile post 4.5, Corolla, Currituck County
May 2010	QI	NC	Currituck County (Not Confirmed)
June 2010	QI	NC	Currituck County (Not Confirmed)
June 25, 2010	NF	NC	In front of Sea Vista Motel, near Beach Access #16, South Topsail Beach, Pender County
June 25, 2010	NF	SC	Fripp Island in Beaufort County
July 17, 2010	NF	NC	Wrightsville Beach in New Hanover County
July 19, 2010	NF	SC	Myrtle Beach in Horry County
July 25, 2010, or July 27, 2010	NF	SC	Isle of Palms in Charleston County
July 2010	NF (SINC)	SC	Otter Island in Charleston County
Aug. 7, 2010	NF	NC	Figure Eight Island in New Hanover County
June 26, 2011	NF	NC	North Topsail Beach in Onslow County
July 19, 2011	NF	NC	Near Ramp 72 in the South Point area of Ocracoke in Hyde County
Aug. 11, 2011	NF	NC	7–10 miles offshore of Beaufort Inlet in Carteret County
Aug. 15, 2011	NF	SC	In the area of 3rd Avenue near the pier, Myrtle Beach in Horry County
Aug. 17, 2011	NF (SINC)	NC	Off Beach Access Number 8 near Moore's Inlet, Wrightsville Beach, New Hanover County
Aug. 17, 2011	NF	NC	Near the H Avenue Beach Access, Kure Beach, New Hanover County

DATE	OUTCOME	AREA	LOCATION
Aug. 24, 2011	NF	NC	Holden Beach in Brunswick County
Aug. 24, 2011	NF	NC	Buxton Beach in Dare County
Sept. 24, 2011	NF	SC	Myrtle Beach in Horry County
Nov. 19, 2011	SE	NC	25 miles southeast of Wrightsville Beach, New Hanover County
May 31, 2012	NF	NC	Hatteras Island, Avon, Outer Banks, Dare County
June 3, 2012	NF (SI)	SC	In the area of 2nd Avenue North, near the pier, Myrtle Beach, Horry County
June 14, 2012	NF	SC	77th Avenue, North Myrtle Beach, Horry County
June 14, 2012	NF	SC	74th Avenue, North Myrtle Beach, Horry County
June 14, 2012	NF (SINC)	SC	82nd Avenue, North Myrtle Beach, Horry County
June 14, 2012	NF	SC	79th Avenue, North Myrtle Beach, Horry County
June 18, 2012	NF	NC	Ocean Isle in Brunswick County
June 19, 2012	NF (SINC)	SC	Myrtle Beach in Horry County
July 8, 2012	NF	NC	North Topsail Beach in Onslow County
July 24, 2012	NF (SINC)	NC	Ocean Isle in Brunswick County
June 14, 2013	NF	SC	Myrtle Beach in Horry County
June 25, 2013	NF	SC	Kiawah Island in Charleston County
July 11, 2013	NF	NC	Holden Beach in Brunswick County
July 30, 2013	NF	SC	Isle of Palms in Charleston County
Aug. 11, 2013	SE	SC	Folly Beach in Charleston County
May 6, 2014	NF	SC	Coligny Beach, Hilton Head Island, Beaufort County
July 3, 2014	NF	SC	Near 10th Street, Isle of Palms, Charleston County
July 12, 2014	NF	NC	Masonboro Inlet in New Hanover County
July 12, 2014	SAPTDU	SC	13 miles southeast of Folly Beach in Charleston County

DATE	OUTCOME	AREA	LOCATION
July 27, 2014	NF (SINC)	NC	11th and 12th Streets, Sunset Beach, Brunswick County
Aug. 6, 2014	NF	SC	Near the 1300 block of East Ashley Road, Folly Beach, Charleston County
Aug. 24, 2014	NF	NC	Masonboro Inlet in New Hanover County
Aug. 26, 2014	NF	NC	Figure Eight Island in New Hanover County
Aug. 27, 2014	NF	SC	Near First Avenue North, Surfside Beach in Horry County
Oct. 14, 2014	NF	SC	Driessen Beach, Hilton Head Island, Beaufort County
May 15, 2015	NF	SC	Sullivan's Island in Charleston County
June 11, 2015	NF	NC	Ocean Isle in Brunswick County
June 14, 2015	NF (SI)	NC	Oak Island in Brunswick County
June 14, 2015	NF (SI)	NC	Oak Island in Brunswick County
June 24, 2015	NF	NC	Surf City in Pender County
June 26, 2015	NF	NC	Hatteras Island, Avon, Outer Banks, Dare County
June 26, 2015	NF	SC	Hunting Island in South Beach, Beaufort County
June 27, 2015	NF (SI)	NC	Rodanthe in Dare County
June 30, 2015	NF	SC	Charleston County Park, Isle of Palms
July 1, 2015	NF	NC	Ocracoke in Hyde County
July 4, 2015	NF	NC	Surf City in Pender County
July 26, 2015	NF	SC	Off Plantation Boulevard, Edisto Island
Aug. 20, 2015	NF	SC	Garden City Beach in Horry County
Sept. 3, 2015	NF	SC	Near 8th Avenue, North Myrtle Beach, Horry County
Oct. 9, 2015	NF	SC	Shipyard Beach Club, Hilton Head Island, Beaufort County
June 7, 2016	SINC	SC	A few blocks from Center Island Fishing Pier, Folly Beach, Charleston County
June 10, 2016	SE	SC	20 miles off Hilton Head Island

DATE	OUTCOME	AREA	LOCATION
June 11, 2016	NF	NC	Atlantic Beach in Carteret County
June 21, 2016	NF	SC	Around 12th Avenue South, North Myrtle Beach, Horry County
June 25, 2016	NF	NC	Just west of the bathhouse at Fort Macon State Park, Atlantic Beach, Carteret County
June 27, 2016	NF	SC	Near Station 22 Street, Sullivan's Island
July 15, 2016	NF	SC	Near 27th Avenue, North Myrtle Beach, Horry County
Sept. 5, 2016	NF	SC	Off Kingston Plantation, Myrtle Beach, Horry County
Sept. 24, 2016	NF	SC	Kiawah Island in Charleston County
Oct. 19, 2016	NF (SINC)	NC	Sound Sea Village in the town of Duck
Feb. 1, 2017	SE	SC	16 miles off Hilton Head Island
March 17, 2017	SE	NC	30 miles offshore of Wrightsville Beach (at 23-Mile Rock)
April 1, 2017	SE	NC	1.73 standard miles (1.5 nautical miles) east of the Oceanana Pier, Atlantic Beach, Carteret County
April 20, 2017	NF	SC	DeBordieu Beach, near Pawleys Island, Georgetown County
April 29, 2017	NF	SC	Near 1655 East Ashley Avenue, Folly Beach, Charleston County
May 30, 2017	NF	SC	1 mile off the Awendaw Landing, Charleston County
June 18, 2017	NF	SC	Near Hilton Head Island, Beaufort County
June 29, 2017	NF	SC	Hilton Head Island in Beaufort County
June 29, 2017	NF (Pro)	NC	Johnnie Mercers Fishing Pier, Wrightsville Beach, New Hanover County
July 11, 2017	NF	SC	Singleton Beach on Hilton Head Island
July 20, 2017	NF (SINC)	SC	South Forest Beach on Hilton Head Island
July 29, 2017	NF	SC	DeBordieu Beach, near Pawleys Island, Georgetown County

DATE	OUTCOME	AREA	LOCATION
July 29, 2017	NF	SC	DeBordieu Beach, near Pawleys Island, Georgetown County
July 29, 2017	NF	SC	Sea Pines Beach on Hilton Head Island
Aug. 9, 2017	NF (SINC)	SC	In front of the Sea Side Resort at South Forest Beach Drive, Hilton Head Island
Aug. 10, 2017	NF	SC	Sea Pines Resort on Hilton Head Island
Aug. 10, 2017	NF	SC	Palmetto Dunes Oceanfront Resort on Hilton Head Island in Beaufort County
Aug. 13, 2017	NF	SC	South Forest Beach on Hilton Head Island
Aug. 30, 2017	SE	NC	Surf City in Pender County
May 13, 2018	NF (SI)	SC	In front of the Disney Beach House on Hilton Head Island in Beaufort County
May 21, 2018	NF	SC	Isle of Palms in Charleston County
July 2, 2018	NF (SINC)	SC	1306 North Ocean Boulevard, Myrtle Beach, Horry County
Aug. 5, 2018	NF	NC	On the east side of Bald Head Island in Brunswick County
Aug. 19, 2018	NF	NC	In front of the Dunes Club, Oceanana Pier Two, Atlantic Beach, Carteret County
June 2, 2019	NF (SI)	NC	Fort Macon State Park, Atlantic Beach, Carteret County
June 10, 2019	NF	NC	Ocean Isle in Brunswick County
June 16, 2019	NF	NC	Bald Head Island in Brunswick County
July 16, 2019	NF	NC	Sunset Beach in Brunswick County
July 30, 2019	NF (Pro)	NC	Off Cape Hatteras in Dare County
Sept. 15, 2019	NF	SC	Isle of Palms in Charleston County

ACKNOWLEDGMENTS

Thank you—

I first want to thank my loving wife Terri Creswell for your support and for putting up with all the long hours that took me away from you to create this work. I also want to thank my parents—Charles Creswell ("Dad") [02/29/1930–08/07/2018] and Libby Creswell ("Mother") for your love, care, and support always. I thank Cary Duncan ("Sister") for the many, many long hours that you freely gave of your time and talents toward perfecting this volume of work. Your professional editing abilities, valuable suggestions as a reader, and creative ideas certainly helped shape this book into what it is. I also thank Chris Creswell ("Brother") for always being just a phone call away. My thanks also go to Warren Arnold ("Grandad") [01/14/1907–06/09/2007] and Marie Arnold ("Grandmother") [12/08/1910–02/07/2012].

I thank Marie Levine for the encouragement to write this book; Aurora X. Bell, Kerri Tolan, and Kathleen Halverson for their professional editing job; and Elise Pullen for the illustrations and Emma Dooling for the indexing. I thank each and every shark bite survivor and the families who allowed me to interview them for this ongoing study of shark–human interactions. I would like to thank the staff of the Shark Research Institute as well as the dedicated people behind the Global Shark Attack File and the International Shark Attack File. My thanks also go to the staff at the University of South Carolina Press; Dr. Daniel Abel; my anonymous peer reviewers; Ralph S. Collier; Dr. Erich K. Ritter (12/08/1958–08/29/2020); Dr. Gordon Hubbell; Dr. Frank J. Schwartz (11/20/1929–11/26/2018); George H. Burgess; Dr. Charles Bangley; Craig Anthony Ferreira; Al Brenneka; Kendra Gerlach; David Batterson; Larry Gurganious; Shirley Maxwell; Donald Millus; Dr. MGF Gilliland; Alexia Morgan; Stanley Kite; Scott Woodard; Kevin Zorc; Ann M. Graham; Kenny Balance;

Victoria Spechko; Jason Banks; Gene Alvarez; Lori Ann Palisi; Julie Howard; Cathy Creswell; Casey and Spencer Creswell; Elsie Creswell; Christian and Morgan Creswell; Bob Duncan; Dr. Jay and Lauren Duncan ("§ection"); Matt Duncan; Faith Taintor; Betty Barbee; David and Samantha Jones; Noah Jones (for loving to hunt shark teeth with me); Joey and Katy Treto; Chris Canipe; Chris Scarboro; Brock Sanders ("Dee"); Shay Nelson (for giving me my first copy of *Shark Attack* by H. David Baldridge); Bill Rudicil; Brad Sherill; Mike Phillips; Sara Jablonski; Tina Croom; Todd Simpson; Alan and Vicki Sewell; Karen Hyatt; Tony Franklin; Pastor Kenny Chinn and Northside Church; The Pender County Health Department; The Pender County Register of Deeds; Jim and Martha Bellizzi; James and Melissa Teachey; Todd Bostian ("Tooth Hunter"); Aaron Palmer ("Grains"); Harry Lewis; Jay and Sharon Willoughby; Brian Martin; Berry Trice, Esq.; Russell D. Nugent, Esq.; Jason Rosenfeld; Kevin Wayne Smith; Andrea Dingeldein; Hailey Winslow; David Capps; Amanda Erickson; Dumeetha Luthra; the National Geographic Channel Network International; the National Geographic Channel Network U.S.A., and The Eye of Every Storm.

There is the sea, vast and spacious, . . . teeming with creatures beyond number . . . living things both large and small.

Psalm 104:25

NOTES

Chapter 1

1. Schwartz, J. Frank, *Sharks, Skates, and Rays of the Carolinas* (Chapel Hill, NC: The University of North Carolina Press, 2003), 1; and Farmer, Charles H., III, *Sharks of South Carolina* (Charleston, SC: Department of Natural Resources, Marine Resources Division, 2004), 8.
2. National Ocean Service, "Why Should We Care About the Ocean?" https://oceanservice.noaa.gov/facts/why-care-about-ocean.html.
3. Schwartz, *Sharks, Skates, and Rays*, 22–25.
4. Schwartz, "History of the Poor Boy Shark Tournament in North Carolina," *Journal of the Elisha Mitchell Scientific Society* 114, no. 3 (July 23, 1998): 149–58.
5. Donald Millus, "Big-Game Fishing's Greatest Catch," *Outdoor Life* (April 1984), in *Tales of Woods and Waters: An Anthology of Classic Hunting and Fishing Stories*, ed. Vin T. Sparano (New York: Skyhorse, 2015).
6. www.southfloridasharkclub.com/foro/viewtopic.php?t=1094

Chapter 2

1. Jay Barnes, "The Sharks of Summer," *Wildlife in North Carolina* 72, no. 8 (August 2007); "NC Beaches Shut as Sharks Close in," *Washington Post*, August 10, 1980, https://www.washingtonpost.com/archive/politics/1980/08/10/nc-beaches-shut-as-sharks-close-in/8c209ffc-9eef-4ed2-a7fd-7c457ac8ab89/?utm_term=.f1c30ca365cd.
2. United States Lifesaving Association, "Statistics," http://arc.usla.org/Statistics/public.asp.
3. Kate Elizabeth Queram, "N.C. Waters 4th Most Deadly for Swimmers in U.S.," *StarNews Online* (Wilmington, NC), February 1, 2014, https://www.starnewsonline.com/article/NC/20140201/News/605028818/WM.
4. Michael J. Patetta, "Drowning Deaths in North Carolina," *SCHS Studies*, no. 42 (August 1986).
5. Jessica Eggert, "Oceans Aren't Swimming Pools: Why Sharks Are Biting North Carolina Beachgoers," *Mashable*, July 5, 2011, https://mashable.com/2015/07/05/north-carolina-shark-attacks/.

6. E. Cortés et al., *Stock Assessment of Dusky Shark in the U.S. Atlantic and Gulf of Mexico* (National Oceanic and Atmospheric Administration Sustainable Fisheries Division, 2006), http://citeseerx.ist.psu.edu/viewdoc /download?doi=10.1.1.178.2791&rep=rep1&type=pdf.
7. "Endangered Shark Species," The Shark Foundation (citing IUCN Red List database), last modified January 10, 2005), https://www.shark.ch /Database/EndangeredSharks/index.html?lim=1&slang=2.
8. "How, Where & When Sharks Attack," Florida Museum of Natural History, last modified December 3, 2019, https://www.floridamuseum.ufl .edu/shark-attacks/odds/how-where-when/.

Chapter 3

1. "How to Avoid Becoming Shark Bait: Two Decades of Shark Attacks," Safewise, last modified July 22, 2019, https://www.safewise.com/blog /decade-of-shark-attacks/.
2. Charles H. Farmer III, *Sharks of South Carolina,* 8.
3. George H. Burgess, Felipe C. Carvalho, and Fábio Hazin, "A Shark Attack Outbreak Off Recife, Pernambuco Brazil: 1992–2006," *Bulletin of Marine Science–Miami* 82, no. 2 (March 2008): 199–212.
4. Charles W. Bangley et al., "Increased Abundance and Nursery Habitat Use of the Bull Shark (*Carcharhinus leucas*) in Response to a Changing Environment in a Warm-Temperate Estuary," *Scientific Reports* 8, article no. 6018 (April 16, 2018).
5. Tess Sheets, "Was It a Shark? This Is How Experts Identify Shark Bites," *TCPalm* (Treasure Coast, FL), July 24, 2018.

Chapter 4

1. Kenneth J. Goldman, "Regulation of Body Temperature in the White Shark, *Carcharodon carcharias,*" *Journal of Comparative Physiology B* 167, no. 6 (January 1997): 423–29, https://doi.org/10.1007/s003600050092.
2. Perry W. Gilbert, *Sharks and Survival* (Boston: D.C. Heath, 1963).
3. J. E. Randall, "Size of the Great White Shark," *Science* 181, no. 4095 (July 13, 1973): pp. 169–70.
4. Vic Hislop, *Shark Man* (Vic Hislop, 1992), 34–36.
5. Susan Casey, *The Devil's Teeth: A True Story of Obsession and Survival Among America's Great White Sharks* (New York: Henry Holt, 2005).
6. Craig Anthony Ferreira, "Largest Whites," Shark-L archives #529, August 30, 2002. You can read more about the Submarine in Craig Ferreira's book, *The Submarine: The True Story of a Giant Great White Shark* and Theo Ferreira's book, *Sharkman: My Obsession with the Great White Shark.*

7. Jon Coen, "Understanding 'Celebrity' Great White Shark Mary Lee," *Grindtv.com*, June 9, 2017.
8. Bill Reaves, "Sharks of the Cape Fear Area and the Atlantic Coast: Excerpt from Beaufort Record," *Wilmington (NC) Weekly Star*, May 5, 1888, Bill Reaves Collection, New Hanover County Library.
9. Frank J. Schwartz, *Sharks of the Carolinas* (University of North Carolina Institute of Marine Sciences, 1989); John Hairr, *Shark! Great White Sharks of the Carolinas and Georgia* (Wilmington, NC: Dram Tree Books, 2009); and Frank J. Schwartz and H. George Burgess, *Sharks of North Carolina and Adjacent Waters* (North Carolina Department of Natural and Economic Resources, Division of Marine Fisheries, 1975).
10. John Hairr, *Shark! Great White Sharks of the Carolinas and Georgia* (Wilmington, NC: Dram Tree, 2009).
11. Glenn Smith, "Sighting of Tooth Giant Stuns 2 Local Fishermen," *Post and Courier* (Charleston, SC), January 4, 2004.
12. Wayne Carter and Dottie Wikan, "Fisherman Catch 3,000 Pound Shark, on Tape, off North Carolina," WVEC.com, May 21, 2004.
13. Shannan Bowen, "Great White Shark Spotted Off Wrightsville Beach," *StarNews Online* (Wilmington, NC), November 11, 2009, https://www.starnewsonline.com/article/NC/20091111/News/605066652/WM.
14. John Hairr, *Shark! Great White Sharks of the Carolinas and Georgia* (Wilmington, NC: Dram Tree, 2009).
15. "Shark Makes Try to Overturn Boat of Marine Giggers," *Beaufort (SC) Gazette*, October 8, 1959.
16. This and the following five encounters are cited in Hairr, *Shark!*
17. John Hairr, *Big Sharks of the Carolina Coast* (Fayetteville, NC: Averasboro Press, 2003).
18. This and the following four encounters are cited in Hairr, *Shark!*
19. Larry Cheek, "A Scare at the Beach," *Fayetteville (NC) Observer*, June 14, 1989.
20. Pat Robertson, "Great White Caught Off SC Coast Not So Great," *The State* (Columbia, SC), July 11, 1993.
21. This and the following four encounters are cited in Hairr, *Shark!*
22. Todd Pusser, "The King of Sharks," *Wildlife in North Carolina* 69, no. 7 (July 2005).
23. Bryan Woodard, "GW Dies on North Carolina Beach," *Shark-L Archives*, December 13, 1998.
24. Hairr, *Shark!*
25. Unofficial report by A. Scott Keen, rescue/EAN diver, certified 1988, July 21, 2001.
26. This and the following two encounters are cited in Hairr, *Shark!*

27. Associated Press, "Video Captures Great White Shark off NC Coast," *StarNews Online* (Wilmington, NC), November 30, 2011, https://www.starnewsonline.com/news/20111130/video-captures-great-white-shark-off-nc-coast.

28. Helen Holt, "Great White Washes Ashore in Wrightsville Beach," WWAY 3 (Wilmington, NC), December 7, 2015, https://www.wwaytv3.com/2015/12/07/great-white-washes-ashore-in-wrightsville-beach/.

29. "Coast Guard Spots Great White Shark Eating Off Beaufort Inlet," WITN (Greeneville, NC), March 23, 2016, https://www.witn.com/content/news/Coast-Guard-spots-great-white-shark-eating-off-Beaufort-Inlet-373255521.html.

30. "Great White Shark Bites Boat Off Hilton Head," WLTX News 19 (Columbia, SC), February 3, 2017, https://www.wltx.com/article/features/great-white-shark-bites-boat-off-hilton-head/101-396249133.

31. Debra Dolan, "Fisherman's Shark Encounter: 'I Freaked Out When I Looked into the Huge Black Eye," WECT News 6 (Wilmington, NC), March 28, 2017, https://www.wect.com/story/35014205/fishermans-shark-encounter-i-freaked-out-when-i-looked-into-the-huge-black-eye/.

32. Mike Shutak, "Fishermen Sight Great White Shark," *Carteret County (NC) News-Times*, April 7, 2017, https://www.carolinacoastonline.com/news_times/article_05216bc6-1b99-11e7-867f-6fc8c2bd953c.html.

33. Natalie Evans, "Teacher 'eaten alive by great white shark as he spearfished with friends in South Australia,'" *The Mirror* (London, UK), September 30, 2015, https://www.mirror.co.uk/news/world-news/teacher-eaten-alive-great-white-6543763.

34. Dipka Bhambhani, "Large Scale Catch: 10-Year-Old Hooks 1,200-Pound Tiger Shark," *Knight Ridder Newspapers*, July 17, 1997.

35. Bill Reaves, "Man Eating Shark Killed Off Coast," *Wilmington (NC) News*, July 13, 1931, Bill Reaves Collection, New Hanover County Library.

36. Amanda Wilcox, "1,200 Pound Tiger Shark Tracked in Cape Fear River," Spectrum News 1 (Coastal NC), June 11, 2015, https://spectrumlocalnews.com/nc/triad/news/2015/06/11/tiger-shark-makes-appearance-in-cape-fear-river.

37. J. A. Musick, *Shark Attack in Virginia: A Report to the Governor's Task Force, Virginia Marine Resource Report No. 2001-14* (Virginia Institute of Marine Science, 2001).

38. Al Brenneka, "Re: 09/12/2009 Richard A. Snead (North Carolina) ***Fatal***," January 11, 2010, *Shark Attack Survivors.com News Archive*,

https://www.sharkattacksurvivors.com/shark_attack/viewtopic.php
?f=44&t=1299&p=2076&hilit=Richard+allen+Sneed#p2076.

39. Allison Feldman, "Teacher Missing from Boat Off Wrightsville," *Wilmington (NC) Morning Star/Sunday Star News*, October 10, 1989.

40. Allison Feldman, "Coast Guard Finds Missing Divers Boat," *Wilmington (NC) Morning Star/Sunday Star News*, October 11, 1989; Joe Swift, "Missing Man's Boat," *Wilmington (NC) Morning Star/Sunday Star News*, October 12, 1989.

41. Allison Feldman, "Search Goes on for Missing Diver," *Wilmington (NC) Morning Star/Sunday Star News*, October 13, 1989; Feldman, "Search for Missing Diver Is Suspended," *Wilmington (NC) Morning Star/Sunday Star News*, October 14, 1989.

42. Personal communication with New Hanover County, North Carolina, search-and-rescue diver.

43. Allison Feldman, "Expert Identifies Body as Nunnally," *Wilmington (NC) Morning Star/Sunday Star News*, October 17, 1989.

44. Personal communication with Professor Frank J. Schwartz.

45. Douglas Gray Nunnally, *Medical Examiner's Certificate of Death*, North Carolina Department of Human Resources, Division of Health Services, Vital Records Branch.

46. Brad Weier, "Shark Mauls Horse," *Queensland [Australia] Times*, March 23, 2005, https://www.qt.com.au/news/apn-shark-mauls/83637/; Pete Thomas, "Rare Footage Shows Clash Between Bull Shark and Angry Hippos," *Men's Journal*, October 15, 2015, https://www.mensjournal.com/adventure/rare-footage-shows-clash-between-bull-shark-and-angry-hippos/.

47. *Topsail Online Gazette*, "Wow . . . is all we can say! A bull shark was pulled out of the water along the Morehead City, North Carolina waterfront on Monday measuring almost 9 feet in length and weighing over 400 pounds!" Facebook, August 22, 2018, https://www.facebook.com/TopsailOnlineGazette/photos/a.1573792066199319/2167907000121153/?type=3&theater.

48. Jerry Dilsaver, "Saltwater Series: The Neuse River," *North Carolina Sportsman*, August 1, 2011, http://www.northcarolinasportsman.com/stories/ncs_mag_1998.htm; Guest Writer, "Tagging Bull Sharks in the Neuse River," *Southern Fried Science*, August 4, 2011, http://www.southernfriedscience.com/tagging-sharks-in-the-neuse-river/.

49. Josh Birch, "Researchers Say Sharks Present in Inland Waterways," WNCT (Greenville, NC), June 16, 2015, https://www.wnct.com/news/researchers-say-sharks-present-in-inland-waterways/.

50. Frances Fountain Shaw and Annie Fountain, *The Tragic Death of Jere Wilson Fountain II: The John R. Fountain Family of Onslow County, North Carolina* (Raleigh, NC: M. T. Fountain, 1992); "Attack by Shark Kills Swimmer off N.C. Coast," *Daily Times News* (Burlington, NC), September 23, 1935; "Shark's Bite Is Fatal to New River Swimmer," *News & Observer* (Raleigh, NC), September 23, 1935.

51. Associated Press, "Apparent Shark Attack Hospitalizes Woman," *Charlotte (NC) Observer,* August 18, 1993; Lane DeGregory, "Shark Attack Called a First in Inland Water / 7-Foot Bull Shark Mauled," *Virginian-Pilot* (Norfolk, VA), August 20, 1993.

52. Trudi Bird, "South Carolina Boy Survives Shark Attack During Surfing Competition," *New York Daily News,* August 13, 2013, https://www .nydailynews.com/news/national/boy-survives-shark-attack-surfing -competition-article-1.1425262.

53. Moni Basu, "After the Shark Bite: How One Boy Inspired Us," CNN, August 21, 2015, https://www.cnn.com/2015/08/21/us/one-boys-courage -in-summer-of-shark-attacks/index.html.

54. Coppleson, Victor, and Peter Goadby. *Shark Attack: How, Why, When & Where Sharks Attack Humans* (rev. ed.). North Ryde, New South Wales, Australia: Angus & Robertson, 1968. p. 198.

55. "Shark Killed Marine Who Fled in Fear," *The Miami News,* August 3, 1960, 11A.

Chapter 5

1. Michael H. A. Piette and Els. A De Letter, "Drowning: Still a Difficult Autopsy Diagnosis," *Forensic Science International* 163, nos. 1–2 (November 10, 2006): 1–9, https://doi.org/10.1016/j.forsciint.2004.10.027.

2. *Wilmington (NC) Star-News,* "Swimmer Missing at Wrightsville Beach Remains a Mystery," *Times-News,* August 4, 2016, https://www.the timesnews.com/news/20160804/swimmer-missing-at-wrightsville -beach-remains-mystery.

3. F. T. Norton, "Swimmer Missing At Wrightsville Beach Remains a Mystery," *Wilmington (NC) Star News,* August 3, 2016.

4. Kazuhiro Nakaya, "A Fatal Attack by a White Shark in Japan and a Review of Shark Attacks in Japanese Waters," *Japanese Journal of Ichthyology* 40, no. 1 (1993): 35–42, https://doi.org/10.11369/jji1950.40.35.

5. Adam Parker, "Surfer Vanishes Off Folly; Authorities Say They Will Resume Search Today," *Post and Courier* (Charleston, SC), September 12, 2005.

6. "Father Recounts Moments Before Son Went Missing During Dive," WCSC Live 5 News (lowcountry SC), July 14, 2014, https://www.live5

news.com/story/26016487/father-recounts-moments-before-son
-went-missing-during-dive/; Natalie Caula Huff, "Remains of Missing
James Island Teenage Diver Recovered [. . .]," *Post and Courier* (Charleston, SC), July 23, 2014, https://www.postandcourier.com/archives
/remains-of-missing-james-island-teenage-diver-recovered-prayers
-for-tristen-allen-family-friends-on/article_5de7a969-0fe5-50d7-b170
-c7c0095c94f9.html.
7. Jenny Sanborn, "Coroner: Missing Diver's Remains Found," ABC News 4
(lowcountry SC), July 24, 2014, https://abcnews4.com/archive/coroner
-missing-divers-remains-found.

Chapter 6

1. Jacques-Yves Cousteau, *The Shark: Splendid Savage of the Sea* (New York:
Doubleday, 1970).
2. "Youngsters Bag Big Shark While Fishing in Sound," *Reno (NV) Evening
Gazette*, August 25, 1936; "Two Attacked by School of 10 Maneaters,"
Charlotte Observer/Parade of Youth (Charlotte, NC), November 1, 1936,
p. 2.

Chapter 7

1. Taylor Smith, "Sustaining Sharks Worldwide: The Shark Research Institute of Princeton," *Princeton Magazine* (2017 blog post), http://www
.princetonmagazine.com/sustaining-sharks-worldwide-the-shark
-research-institute-of-princeton/.
2. Marie Levine, "The Global Shark Attack File," *Shark Info International
Media Services: Research News and Background Information on the Protection, Ecology, Biology, and Behavior of Sharks*, February 15, 1999, https://
www.sharkinfo.ch/SI1_99e/gsaf.html.

FURTHER READING

Websites

Shark Research Institute: www.sharks.org.

Global Shark Attack File: www.sharkattackfile.net/.

International Shark Attack File: https://www.floridamuseum.ufl.edu
/shark-attacks/.

Books

Abel, Daniel C., and R. Dean Grubbs. *Shark Biology and Conservation: Essentials for Educators, Students, and Enthusiasts.* Baltimore: Johns Hopkins University Press, 2020.

Allen, Thomas B. *Shark Attacks: Their Causes and Avoidance.* New York: Lyons Press, 2001.

Baldridge, H. David. *Shark Attack.* Anderson, SC: Droke House/Hallux, 1974.

Benchley, Peter. *Shark Trouble.* New York: Random House, 2002.

Capuzzo, Michael. *Close to Shore: The Terrifying Shark Attacks of 1916.* New York: Broadway Books, 2002.

Casey, Susan. *The Devil's Teeth: A True Story of Obsession and Survival Among America's Great White Sharks.* New York: Henry Holt, 2005.

Cocke, Joe. *Fossil Shark Teeth of the World: A Collector's Guide.* Torrance, CA: Lamna Books, 2002.

Collier, Ralph S. *Shark Attacks of the Twentieth Century: From the Pacific Coast of North America.* Bristol, UK: Scientia, 2003.

Coppleson, Victor, and Peter Goadby. *Shark Attack: How, Why, When & Where Sharks Attack Humans* (rev. ed.). North Ryde, New South Wales, Australia: Angus & Robertson, 1968.

Ellis, Richard, and John E. McCosker. *Great White Shark: The Definitive Look at the Most Terrifying Creature of the Ocean.* Redwood City, CA: Stanford University Press, 1991.

Farmer. *Sharks of South Carolina.* Charleston, SC: Department of Natural Resources, Marine Resources Division, 2004.

Fernicola, Richard G. *Twelve Days of Terror: Inside the Shocking 1916 New Jersey Shark Attacks*. New York: Lyons Press, 2016.

Goldstein, Robert. *Coastal Fishing in the Carolinas: From Surf, Pier, and Jetty*. Durham, NC: John F. Blair, 1988.

Hairr, John. *Big Sharks of the Carolina Coast*. Fayetteville, NC: Averasboro Press, 2003.

Hairr, John. *Shark! Great White Sharks of the Carolinas and Georgia*. Wilmington, NC: Dram Tree Books, 2009.

Klimley, A. Peter, and David G. Ainley. *Great White Sharks: The Biology of Carcharodon Carcharias*. London: Harcourt, Brace, 1996.

MacCormick, Alex. *Shark Attacks: Terrifying True Accounts of Shark Attacks Worldwide*. New York: Constable, 1998.

Reid, Robert. *Shark! Killer Tales From the Dangerous Depths*. Crows Nest, New South Wales, Australia: Allen & Unwin, 2010.

Scharp, Hal. *Shark Safari*. New York: A. S. Barnes, 1975.

Schwartz, Frank J. *Sharks, Skates, and Rays of the Carolinas*. Chapel Hill: The University of North Carolina Press, 2003.

Articles

Bangley, Charles. "Sharks of North Carolina." *Coastwatch*, Spring 2014. https://ncseagrant.ncsu.edu/coastwatch/previous-issues/2014-2/spring -2014/sharks-of-north-carolina/.

Burgess, George. "The Science of Shark Attacks." *Outside Online*, December 18, 2012. https://www.outsideonline.com/1911871/george-burgess -science-shark-attacks.

International Shark Attack File. "Yearly Worldwide Shark Attack Summary." https://www.floridamuseum.ufl.edu/shark-attacks/yearly-world wide-summary/.

Schwartz, Frank J. "Bull Sharks in North Carolina." *Journal of the North Carolina Academy of Science* 128, no. 3/4 (Fall/Winter 2012): 88–91. https:// doi.org/10.7572/2167-5880-128.3.88.

INDEX